Women, Borders, and Violence

Sharon Pickering

Women, Borders, and Violence

Current Issues in Asylum, Forced Migration and Trafficking

 Springer

Professor Sharon Pickering
Department of Criminal Justice & Criminology
Monash University
Caulfield East, VIC 3145
Australia
sharon.pickering@arts.monash.edu.au

ISBN 978-1-4419-0270-2   e-ISBN 978-1-4419-0271-9
DOI 10.1007/978-1-4419-0271-9
Springer New York Dordrecht Heidelberg London

Printed on acid-free paper

Springer is part of Springer Science+Business Media (www.springer.com)

Acknowledgements

I am grateful to the colleagues who worked with me on this book—Alison Gerard and Marie Segrave who co-author two of the chapters. I am also indebted to the assistance of Sarah Segal and Mary O'Kane as well as the painstaking work of Julia Farrell. My colleagues at Monash University have, as always, been enormously supportive and generate a wonderful place to work—Jude McCulloch, Dean Wilson, Marie Segrave, JaneMaree Maher, Danielle Tyson, Anna Eriksson and Bree Carlton. I am grateful to team at Crest Premedia Solutions, Pune, India for their patience and care of the manuscript.

This book owes an intellectual debt to the work of Leanne Weber and Nancy Wonders who always improve my thinking and have engaged me on many of the issues explored in this book. Of course, any errors are mine alone.

Parts of Chapter 4 draw on work presented to and published by the International Association of Refugee Law Judges, and some data are reproduced from Pickering and Lambert, *Global Issues, Women and Justice*, published by the Institute of Criminology. Chapter 6 includes excerpts from Pickering, S., 'Transversal Policing' in *The Australian and New Zealand Journal of Criminology* (2004).

My love and thanks to Tom and to my parents for their endless and unwavering support. Wesley and Amelia sat just off my elbows for most of the writing of this book and have shown patience and understanding beyond any reasonable expectation for 2- and 4-years olds—thank you.

Contents

Abbreviations

ABSDF	All Burma Students' Democratic Front
AFM	Armed Forces of Malta
AFP	Australian Federal Police
ANAO	Australian National Audit Office
BWU	Burmese Women's Union
ECRI	European Commission Against Racism and Intolerance
EU	European Union
HRC	Human Rights Council
HRW	Human Rights Watch
IDP	Internally Displaced Persons
ICG	International Crisis Group
ICJ	International Commission of Jurists
IOM	International Organization for Migration
JRS	Jesuit Refugee Service
MFSS	Ministry of Family and Social Services
MJHA	Ministry of Justice and Home Affairs
MSF	Médicins Sans Frontières
NGO	Non-Government Organization
NLD	National League for Democracy
NSO	National Statistics Office
OAU	Organization for African Unity
SPDC	State Peace and Development Council
TIP	Trafficking in Persons
UN	United Nations
UNDP	United Nations Development Program
UNHCR	United Nations High Commissioner for Refugees
UNODC	United Nations Office on Drugs and Crime
UNOSOM	United Nations Operation in Somalia
USCRI	US Committee for Refugees and Immigrants
USDOS	US Department of State

Chapter 1
Women and Extra Legal Border Crossing

Insecurities hover in a circle. Within a secure circle, there are insecure spaces; similarly there are insecure zones at the point where circles meet; within grand security little insecurities persist—little not to those who are insecure but to the custodians of grand security. A feminist perspective suggests a critical view of these grand perceptions, a concern for what passes as the small, and a willingness to stand the existing accounts on their heads. That can be done when women's chronicles have been given priority in accounts of security.

(Banerjee, 2010)

Even the freest of free societies is unfree at the edge, where things and people go out and other people and things come in. Here, at the edge we submit to scrutiny, to inspection, or judgement. These people guarding these lines must tell us who we are. We must be passive, docile. To be otherwise is suspect, and at the frontier to come under suspicion is the worst of all possible crimes....

(Rushdie, 2002)

1 Introduction

For the vast majority of the world's women there is no legal migration from the Global South to the Global North. Yet the absence of legal avenues for migration has not quelled the desire for global mobility—women still move across borders for a range of reasons. The effective target hardening of the wealthiest nations of the world of migrants from the poorest nations of the world has created a new (renewed) frontier of illegality: border crossing. Like many other forms of illegality and the attempts to police them, extra legal border crossing has significant gendered dimensions. This book explores women's extra legal border crossing in the midst of some of the most intractable conflicts and contested border crossing regions of the world. The impossibility of legally crossing many borders is not specific to the experience of women. However, the experience of extra legal crossing is significantly different for women.

S. Pickering, *Women, Borders, and Violence,*
DOI 10.1007/978-1-4419-0271-9_1, © Springer Science+Business Media, LLC 2011

If we were to begin with official accounts of extra legal border crossing—those generated by governments and international agencies—this book would continue down a predictable route of a gendered analysis of border policing that is carried out at broadly recognisable border policing posts: at checkpoints, at airports, during immigration compliance raids, and the like. It would focus on the ways in which border policing is gendered and thus comparable to other policing functions in liberal democracies. However, this book is based on interviews with women from diverse regions of the world about their experiences of fleeing violence, persecution and conflict. It is developed around thick descriptions of extra legal border crossing. It explores the groups and individuals that women themselves identify as policing their border crossings. As such, it redirects this criminological inquiry away from one concerned with a gendered analysis of the ever-growing policing apparatus to one that acknowledges the less linear nature of migration, and the more dispersed forms of policing that impact on women's extra legal border crossings. Exploring the interviews and available evidence this book charts the ways in which violence and criminality control extra legal border crossing, and identifies that one of the most potent forms of this control is gender-based violence. It also considers the plurality of the border policing effort as carried out by webs of state and non-state agents, as well as the increasingly complex international legal apparatus of refugee protection that operates as one of the few "gates" in the border policing fence between the Global South and the Global North.

The development of understandings of borders has come to incorporate a set of broadly identifiable and broadly applicable common ideas: globalisation, sovereignty, human rights, violence, mobility and security, to name just a few. Most of the concern within the social sciences with borders either broadly or specifically addresses these issues in one way or another (see, for example, Donnan & Wilson, 1999; Gready, 2004; Ortiz, 2001; Howitt, 2001; Soguk, 1999; Devetak, 1995). Each one is worthy of significant attention, and taken collectively they represent some of the great intellectual and organisational challenges that have emerged and re-emerged throughout history. The focus on these doctrines or concepts (depending on your position) has necessitated a sweeping analysis of global conditions, including some comparative analysis (see, for example, Sassen, 1998). The existence of such works perhaps begs the question as to why we need local accounts of what may reasonably be viewed as global, or at least regional, phenomena. Moreover, we might ask: what makes women's accounts of extra legal border crossing particularly valuable? The answer is that globalisation or sovereignty or security mean different things to people in Burma or Malta or Australia. Human rights and mobility and violence mean different things to people in Thailand and Somalia and the United States. These differing interpretations and their implications are well understood by women who have either willingly made or been forced to make extra legal border crossings.

For criminologists the local context of such far-reaching phenomena as globalisation, sovereignty and security is particularly meaningful. Criminology has historically concerned itself with crime and criminal justice that is jurisdictionally based, which ordinarily has meant focusing on those crimes and criminal justice responses that occur within territorial nation-states (see Pickering & Weber, 2006). While there have been historical exceptions—the policing of the alien being one (see Finnane, 2009)—the vast bulk of criminological concern has been with the individual and the state within the traditional boundaries of the state. Comprehending the meaning of international and transnational phenomena via the meanings and experiences of mobility, security and human rights for those who have been the targets of exclusion is a predictably criminological approach to the debates. As Nancy Wonders has powerfully demonstrated in her work on migrant women and safety, globalisation always comes to ground somewhere. In this book globalisation comes to ground in Somalia, Malta, Burma and Thailand, and in the United States, the United Kingdom and Australia. As Paula notes at the beginning of this chapter it is through exploring the small spaces that we can understand the ways in which grand securities and insecurities are experienced and the impacts they have on individual lives, communities and nations. Moreover, her understanding of circles of insecurities evidenced by the small stories of women has the potential to challenge grand narratives. In this sense I am informed by my experience of working in Thailand, Malaysia, Hong Kong and the Philippines with Caroline Lambert and Christine Alder, where we learnt that questions about human rights can, on the one hand, lead to rather rigid and flat legal controversies, on the other, to understanding human rights through the stories of women, which results in more complex and exciting legal, cultural and gendered debates. Understanding from the specific to the general will enable engagements across difference. It is also a political decision, as I previously wrote with Lambert and Alder:

> It is no longer acceptable (if it ever has been) to ponder questions of human rights apart from issues of experience or attempts at narration by and with those who are always talked about but never found within esteemed legal and political commentary. (2003, p. 166)

Understanding borders and mobility is bound to be more expansive and complex if it includes the experiences and meanings of violence, security, globalisation and human rights generated by women. This book advances debates around the tensions between globalisation and security, borders and human rights, violence and mobility by referencing the diverse experiences of women.

This book is based on research that is focused on how women experience border policing when they attempt to cross borders extra legally. For a criminologist, border policing is a conceptual and geographical frontier at which to understand the changing nature of law enforcement in the context of globalisation, whereby the bleeding of the internal and external security functions of civilian police and the military renders them increasingly indistinct and realised in increasingly gendered ways. In this book the border is understood as extending far beyond the physical territorial border and into a range of functional border policing moments, both internal and external to the nation-state (see Weber, 2006). The border policing agents of the state effectively constitute a moment, albeit an important moment, in women's experiences of extra legal border crossing.

The Smuggling Protocol to the United Nations (UN) *Convention against Transnational Crime* has escalated the criminalisation of extra legal border crossing and catalysed harmonisation efforts between nations. Prior to the introduction of the Protocol a state could sanction persons found to be unlawfully entering its sovereign territory. Since its implementation there has been an international legal obligation to criminalise all forms of extra legal border crossing. The result of this process of mandatory criminalisation has been heightened levels of border policing and border enforcement cooperation between nations, and "a host of states—including both countries of origin and transit—have been effectively conscripted as agents of first world states of destination" (Hathaway, 2008, p. 27). The effective "contracting out" of migration control to countries of transit and destination relocates the fundamentally political problem of extra legal migrants from wealthy countries to poor countries. The case studies in this book document the ways in which such border policing concerns result in many and varied practices of violence and resistance that are fundamentally shaped by gender.

This book considers extra legal border crossing as a segment of a continuum of border crossing that has no beginning or end. There is a pervasive fiction surrounding the journey from country of origin through border crossing to countries of reception—a fiction that adopts a pre-citizen timeframe, at the end of which migration status is normalised. This book suggests that for many women the transition from pre-citizen to citizen is not only difficult but also simply does not occur, for any meaningful migration status—one that brings rights and privileges—does not exist. This book explores how women's extra legal border crossings occur in contexts of unchecked violence, how borders are policed beyond territorial markers, how policing is enacted by both state and non-state agents, and how border crossing neither begins nor ends with the extra legal crossing of a territorial border.

This chapter explores the criminological basis for understanding women's extra legal border crossing, beginning with the production of knowledge about women's experiences followed by an analysis of the phases of scholarship which may be regarded as informing the chapters that follow and their attempt to exploration of gender, violence and mobility. I turn first to the broad doctrines and concepts that shape this scholarship and in the first instance assist us to make sense of women's local experiences of extra legal border crossing. The chapter then explores the ways in which women's experiences of border crossing, and the meanings they generate, speak of the phenomenon more generally.

In the burgeoning literature on global mobility and security there are multifarious terms used to talk about people who cross borders. There are those who denote the crossing in terms of state definition and sanction (unauthorised arrival), those who use black letter law definitions (such as "asylum seeker" or "refugee"), those who utilise labels that attempt to recognise and assign the relative agency of people who cross borders (including "transnational legal subject" and "transnational migrant actor"), and those who use popular if imprecise labels (such as "economic" or "political migrant"). Because this study is concerned with what happens when a woman crosses a border without the approval of the nation-state the terminology "extra legal border crossing" has been chosen. I recognise that this terminology is perhaps a little cumbersome, but I hope generous readers will identify within this definition a commitment to understanding border crossing primarily as a contravention of state law or policies on particular forms of migration, and an absence of the political loading of terms such as "illegal" or "clandestine". I also hope readers will see that "extra legal" invokes the possibility of legislative change in how we classify those who cross the border without state permission. In short, the term "extra legal" reminds us that it is laws that are capable of change. In various places throughout the chapters of this book the term "refugee" is used for women who have sought to engage the formal national and international protection regime provided by the United Nations *Convention on the Status of Refugees* (the Refugee Convention) and its realisation through various national legislative frameworks. The term "refugee" is used in a general sense when discussing contexts where there has been broad international acceptance of populations or sub-populations as being refugee populations (for example, following the 1988 protests in Burma and following the fall of the Somali Government in the early 1990s).

2   Counting Women's Extra Legal Border Crossing

The official picture of women crossing borders extra legally is complicated and partial. The collection, analysis and distribution of sex-disaggregated data on migration flows, including extra legal flows, is not systematically undertaken by any international or regional institution or agency. Domestic data on women who cross borders extra legally are equally problematic, albeit for additional reasons. Therefore, by global counts or cumulative estimations based on domestic recording, there is a dearth of quantifiable knowledge about women who cross borders extra legally.

Of all women who cross borders extra legally we know more, quantifiably, about women who have been counted and classified as part of the refugee protection and/or assistance regime. For women fleeing persecution, violence and conflict the United Nations High Commissioner for Refugees (UNHCR) paints part of the picture. UNHCR collects and analyses data in relation to the number of women who apply for refugee status through UNHCR, and estimates the overall size of global and regional refugee and internally displaced person (IDP) populations and the percentage of those who are women and children. The UNHCR mandate includes concern for refugees, asylum seekers, returnees, internally displaced persons and stateless persons. In addition, it may include other groups or persons of concern to whom UNHCR has extended its protection or assistance.

UNHCR field offices provide statistics on the number of women who register with them, most notably inside refugee camps. Research on refugee camps has indicated the difficulties many women face in seeing to be registered and hence appearing in the official picture of the camps. Although some figures are kept on the level of violence, including sexual violence, in refugee camps, significant shortcomings are evident in the collection of data. Such deficiencies include camp authorities relying on women to report violence to them (even though authorities may be thin on the ground or themselves perpetrators of violence) or to international agencies that may intermittently leave the camps due to instability or may only open their offices during particular hours, as well as camp authorities only being resourced for particular functions.

In addition, UNHCR provides some disaggregated data by sex for specific geographic or thematic groups. UNHCR also collects, analyses and distributes data on global trends in refugee movements that are broadly analysed on a regional basis, as well as data on asylum levels and global trends in industrialised countries. These annual reporting mechanisms do not disaggregate for gender. In 2001 there appeared a curious anomaly in the organisation's policy. In the annual UNHCR *Statistical Yearbook* of 2001, Chap. 2 is dedicated to an analysis of gender. In this publication the justification for offering a gendered analysis of data included the following:

> Reflecting UNHCR's long-term commitment towards improving gender and age data, the demographic profile is currently available for almost eight million persons compared to less than four million in the mid-1990s. In 2001 some 120 countries reported population data partly or fully disaggregated by gender and age. (UNHCR, 2001, p. 34)

The analysis of these data revealed that the availability of gender profiles was greater in developing countries than in industrialised countries. In short, UNHCR appears to have more robust counting and classificatory schemes in countries where they operate on the ground offering relief and shelter than in countries such as the United States, Australia, Italy and other nations of the Global North where counting and classification remains the remit of the government. Furthermore, the report highlighted that if data collected by UNHCR in developing nations were removed from the global counting of women refugees the developed world could only offer a gender-disaggregated count of less than 7% of the entire refugee population. Curiously, in no year prior to 2001, and no year since, has the UNHCR *Statistical Yearbook* included a gendered analysis, let alone a chapter dedicated to the task.

The collation of refugee statistics has been considered fundamental in the allocation of resources and services for refugee populations (Harrell-Bond, Voutira, & Leopold, 1992). However, UNHCR statistics, even if they were disaggregated by sex, can only be a crude indicator of the number or proportion of women in the refugee population. As Jeff Crisp has detailed, the collection and analysis of refugee statistics are plagued by fundamental problems. These problems include the definitional imprecision of categories such as "refugee" and "asylum seeker", and the dissonance between the policy of UNHCR and its operational imperatives in emergency and conflict situations. Fundamentally, the geographical size of border regions, the mobility of populations (locally and internationally), and the conditions on the ground for those conducting the count all auger against the accuracy and prioritisation of enumeration:

> In several recent refugee crises, very limited numbers of UNHCR field staff have been confronted with movements of half a million refugees or more, across large geographical areas and in some of the most remote, weakly administered and environmentally hostile territories on earth. In such circumstances, the obstacles to effective enumeration are legion. Refugees may enter a country of asylum at numerous different points along a border. They may arrive in such large numbers that they can scarcely be counted. The influx may take place in an area where UNHCR has no access, due to insecurity or governmental obstruction. Some refugees may prefer not to be identified or counted. And UNHCR and its partners may well consider that their limited resources are best spent on the provision of life-saving assistance, rather than on counting the potential beneficiaries. (Crisp, 1999, p. 5)

These challenges have led some to contend that accurately counting refugees is as impossible as it is desirable. Harrell-Bond et al. (1992) have argued that counting refugees is a technocratic effort contributing to a broader ideology of control over refugees in order to ease the burden of delivering aid, in place of the promotion and realisation of refugee rights. As noted by Harrell-Bond and others, the easiest way to count refugees is to physically restrain them within confined spaces. Therefore, efforts at enumeration must be carefully considered.

Governments of the Global North collect and distribute statistics disaggregated by gender relating to people who cross their borders. However, there is significant variation in the availability of data on those who cross borders extra legally. Most countries collect and distribute statistics on people who arrive extra legally by boat, largely because of the political cache currently attached to responding harshly to such arrivals, especially in countries such as Australia and Canada. A breakdown by sex of such arrivals is often only gleaned through media reports. The number of people who arrive by boat who are interdicted and returned to countries of embarkation is not known.

I made formal requests for information from a range of countries regarding the number of women who cross their borders extra legally. Governments were asked for the following information:

1. The number of women who attempted to cross their borders extra legally
2. The number of women who arrived at a land, sea or air port without valid entry documentation
3. The number of women who arrived at a land, sea or air port who were denied entry
4. The number of women who arrived at a land, sea or air port who were detained
5. The number of women who arrived at a land, sea or air port who claimed asylum
6. The number of women who were interdicted in international or extra-territorial waters
7. The number of women who were granted asylum

The only information governments made available related to point 7 above. Unless women are among those granted refugee status, those fleeing conflict and seeking asylum are broadly erased from the numerical picture of women who cross borders. Moreover, the policies and practices of governments explicitly and implicitly prevent researchers from gaining access to data on these populations. As Correa-Velez and Gifford (2007) have argued, "…there is an imperative for liberal democratic governments to guarantee researchers access to unidentified data concerning the most marginalised and vulnerable populations as a matter of course" (p. 279). The outcome of border protection policies coupled with the secrecy of official data results in those who are refused asylum melting into a seemingly invisible class of non-citizens about whom our knowledge is severely limited.

Similarly, the attempt to quantify the number of women trafficked across borders extra legally for work in the sex industry has attracted significant criticism. Estimating the number of women trafficked across borders predominantly for work in the sex industry has resulted in what some researchers have called the "slipperiness of numbers". For example, Segrave, Milivojevic, and Pickering (2009, p. 12) have detailed that the US Department of State's Trafficking in Persons (TIP) Report, widely used as an international reference point, estimated in 2002 that between 700,000 and 4 million people are trafficked annually (USDOS, 2002). In the same year the United Nations Development Program (UNDP) estimated that 1.2 million women are trafficked into the sex industry annually. By 2006, the TIP Report dramatically reduced this count to between 600,000 and 800,000 people, with approximately 80% believed to be women and children (USDOS, 2006). In 1998, the International Organisation for Migration (IOM) estimated that 300,000 women were trafficked to and within Europe, around two-thirds of whom were women and children. In 2000 the IOM increased this estimate to 500,000. The European Commission estimated in 2001 that 120,000 women were trafficked in Europe while the European Union (EU) estimated in 2004 that there were approximately 200,000 women victims of trafficking. These varying estimates in many ways mirror the debates around the extent of the "white slave trade" that emerged almost a century earlier (Segrave et al., 2009).

It has been suggested that no country can produce reliable data to estimate the extent of sex trafficking (Kelly, 2002). For example, in Australia non-government organisations (NGOs) estimate the number of trafficking victims to be, on the one hand, as low as ten and, on the other hand, as high as 100 (see Scarlett Alliance, Project Respect). The Australian Federal Police suggests estimates of around 22 women trafficked into the sex industry in Australia each year. Such examples have led researchers to conclude that the quality and extent of our knowledge of sex trafficking is poor, despite the burgeoning literature on this aspect of women's global migration (legal or extra legal) into the sex industry. A plausible explanation for the problematic estimations of the size and scope of sex trafficking has been the complexity of the practice and experience of the phenomenon. As Segrave et al. have argued, there are good reasons to consider that the understanding, measurement and definition of sex trafficking require critical scrutiny (2009, p. 14). Central to this criticism has been the difficulty of ascribing victim status. Research suggests that women who have been identified as being trafficked may not self-identify as victims. Even if they do engage with the criminal justice system they may not necessarily be "counted" in official crime statistics. The legacy of debates over whether women consent to work in the sex industry, and moralistic attributions of culpability that result from such consent, continue to colour many estimations of who counts as a victim of sex trafficking (Goo   ᵃ⁴) ᵀᵇ   ⁱminal justice and migration-related data also paints   ng, especially in terms of the extent to which the r   introduced to reduce trafficking can be measure   However, the greatest challenge for estimating the extent of sex trafficking is that it has become almost invisible at the patrolled national border. Women who do experience sex trafficking are increasingly crossing borders using their own passports and valid visas, under the control of increasingly sophisticated trafficking networks utilising high-quality false documentation, or are being subject to internal trafficking. The focus on trafficking has produced sets of numbers that at best are slippery and at worst fictitious and subject to politicisation informed by determinations of the legitimacy of sex work.

What these examples and other forms of women's extra legal border crossing suggest is that the collection, analysis and distribution of data are fundamentally shaped by the nature of the borders being considered and the politicised production and release of information by both government and non-government agencies. The very nature of the border produces varying opportunities for the production of knowledge. For example, due to its geography and a total visa system Australia can claim to know about all extra legal border crossings that result in arrival on the Australian mainland either by boat or aeroplane. However, what remains unknown are those attempted extra legal crossings that are aborted, fail to arrive at the mainland or are intercepted and turned around. It has recently been identified that in relation to migration across the vast waters between Australia and her nearest neighbour, Indonesia, very little is known about extra legal border crossing and even less about the gender-specific determinants of such experiences. For other nations, porous or semi-porous borders are the norm and therefore extra legal border crossings are easier to undertake, despite the massive fortification of borders, especially around the EU and North America. This presents opportunities for proportions of extra legal border crossings to go largely undetected, beyond the discovery of people in host countries who do not possess the requisite entry documentation.

The deaths of extra legal border crossers have prompted NGOs and governments in some parts of the world to focus their analysis of the border on the harm that it produces. These concerns have largely emanated from Europe and the United States in response to the fortification of borders and what has been regarded as "target hardening". More recently the nascent academic literature on the production of harm at the territorial border has focused on the extent to which the fortification of borders results in deaths and the ways in which death may occur differently for men and women. For example, the US Government under both President Clinton and later under President Bush fortified sections of the US–Mexico border in ways that used the topography of the region to deter border crossing, the harsh Arizona desert a funnel for entry into the United States. However, instead of deterring extra legal crossing this strategy increased the risk of death during crossing and resulted in would-be migrants utilising the services of increasingly sophisticated smuggling networks to cross. Those who could not afford smugglers were found to be at greater risk of harm and death in the heat of the day or the cold of the night. Forensic anthropologists have found that women who have sought to make this crossing die more quickly and of more painful deaths.

3 Women's Extra Legal Border Crossing

Considering the breadth and depth of scholarship on migration there is a dearth of scholarship on women's extra legal border crossing. As noted above, the official picture renders women's extra legal border crossing almost invisible. However, research efforts in this area are shaped by earlier phases of scholarship that attempted to recover women in the international literature on violence and migration.

The first phase of relevant scholarship has been concerned broadly with violence against women, and has overwhelmingly centred its analysis on the state. Driven by tireless campaigning on the part of the NGO sector, this literature has underpinned the broader struggle for the international recognition of women's human rights and a recalibration of the international legal and human rights canon to include women's experiences. This has been an important and pivotal body of scholarship which has highlighted women's struggles for change and within which we can identify the burgeoning literature on gender and refugee law. The gendered violence of conflict, particularly the use of rape and sexual violence by military personnel, has spawned a vast and compelling body of literature and resulted in key victories in the international legal realm which have rendered women's experiences of violence important to understanding the nature, and redressing the impact of conflict and violence. However, gendered violence continues to be effectively precluded from broader theorisations around security and violence, especially in the field of international relations (Shepherd, 2007). Criminological accounts that draw on the scholarship on violence against women and extra legal border crossing are all but absent. The most relevant components of the violence against women literature are grounded in ethnographic accounts of the border, focus on local and regional contexts, and are dominated by those concerned with trafficking.

4 Trafficking

The second identifiable phase of scholarship is the vast and noisy literature on trafficking, which has overwhelmingly become the international focus of research on women crossing borders. More specifically this literature has focused on trafficking into the sex industry. The impact of much of this research has been to delimit women's opportunity for border crossing, to expand the security and policing apparatus of the state, and to infantilise or demonise those women it purportedly seeks to rescue or defend. Trafficking research has significantly contributed towards broadbrush criminalisation of women who cross borders, heightened the importance of prosecutorial efforts and recrafted the scope of enforcement agencies.

The sex trafficking debates gained prominence after the development of the Trafficking Protocol to the UN *Convention against Organized Crime* and its focus on border control. While several elements of the Protocol continue to be subject to debate among various protagonists working in the field of sex trafficking, there is a growing body of scholarship, both inside and outside criminology, that points to the fundamental tension between the Protocol and human rights goals, and highlights the collateral damage that the Protocol promotes. The Protocol is concerned with trans-border movement that requires broad criminalisation, and incorporates smuggling, which has ordinarily been of a different nature, scope and impact to trafficking activities. As Hathaway (2008, p. 5) has argued, "…most smuggling has historically been a consensual and relatively benign market-based response to the existence of laws that seek to artificially constrain the marriage of surplus labor supply on one side of a border with an unmet demand for certain forms of labor on the other side of the border". Hathaway concludes that it is reasonable to expect that the criminalisation of smuggling will increase the risk of trafficking insofar as it will inflate the cost of assisted movement across borders, "leaving the poor with no choice but to mortgage their futures in order to pay for safe passage" (2008, p. 5). The Protocol requires states to implement programs aimed at preventing a range of cross-border movements, which are essentially based on the pre-emption of crime and on forms of profiling likely victims and pre-empting their potential victimisation (Milivojevic & Pickering, 2008).

For criminologists, trafficking represents a foothold of relevance in the world of extra legal migration because, unlike traditional conceptions of extra legal migration, trafficking has criminal victims. Of course this is premised on those trafficked as "deserving" of the label victim. The evidence overwhelmingly indicates that border policing (as traditionally conceived) has been an inadequate site for identifying victims of trafficking. Moreover, increasing evidence suggests that women trafficked do not cross borders extra legally, and therefore the policing they experience is predominantly shaped by the disposition of regulatory regimes around sex work and their enforcement and compliance, rather than by the border policing edifice (which instead largely functions as the sting in the tail of an already elaborate, albeit impotent, legal response). Analysis of the Trafficking Protocol has led to the argument that it does not equate trafficking with exploitation, and therefore no obligation flows from the Protocol to do anything about exploitation or provide any remedy for redress for those exploited (Hathaway, 2008). Trafficking absorbs the attention of academics and exploits, on the one hand, the ambivalence of most Western nations about prostitution and, on the other, the fervour with which nations embrace the opportunity to display their security credentials by ideologically and materially resourcing agencies to identify and rescue victims and prosecute offenders, despite evidence suggesting that success has not been achieved on either front.

5   The Feminisation of Survival

The third relevant phase of scholarship relates to the feminisation of survival, which has captured the imagination of many, particularly in the fields of sociology and anthropology and to a lesser extent economics. Broadly informed by the work of Saskia Sassen, this literature has focused on women in the global economy and in particular their unregulated labour and precarious migration status. Sassen has made a compelling case that under conditions of globalisation fundamental properties of the nation-state, notably exclusive territoriality and sovereignty, have been reconfigured (1998, p. 81) to produce new regulatory and legal regimes. Questioning the role of women in the global economy, Sassen has argued that women may be regarded as new international actors, and challenges historical ideas around the sovereign nation-state. Replete with examples drawn from a range of zones in which economic migration has become an intensely gendered practice, this scholarship has compelled analyses to locate gender at the centre of understandings of new incarnations of the global economic system and the drivers of migratory processes. The gendered economics of migration generates questions connected to understanding the related but distinct experience of those fleeing persecution, which is broadly informed by conflict and gendered violence rather than economic opportunity and resource scarcity. This is not to suggest a hierarchy of motivations for extra legal border crossing, but rather that the experience of extra legal border crossers may have particular characteristics for those migrating for divergent, albeit related, reasons.

6   Border Policing

Border policing is not new. Border policing as a law enforcement function has been of historical and contemporary interest to criminologists focused on the criminalisation of migration and the criminalisation of "alien" others. Furthermore, the relationship between migration and crime has been an abiding interest for criminologists. Historically that concern has revolved around the criminal behaviour of migrants and their propensity in various generations and contexts to commit particular kinds of crimes. Some of the most seminal criminological work on the study of deviance has focused on migrant neighbourhoods and families. Unsurprisingly, an area of criminological inquiry emerged that explored the policing of such groups and their experiences of the criminal justice system, and often focused on issues of inequality, disadvantage and racism. Interestingly, it took some decades for criminological interest to shift from a focus on criminal behaviour and criminal justice responses towards the interdependence of immigration and the criminal justice system. Initially, this criminological interest focused on the use of enforcement at the territorial border, particularly at ports, and the often-unchecked practices of state agents (see, for example, Weber & Gelsthorpe, 2000). Relatively quickly attention turned to de-centring the territorial nation-state in order to understand the intersection of national security and criminal justice concerns in relation to increasingly mobile territorial borders (Weber & Bowling 2004; Weber 2006). The work of Weber & Bowling 2004; Weber 2006 has redefined how criminologists understand border policing by detailing the many internal and external borders that are effectively policed by state and non-state agents in ways that shore up the integrity of the sovereign nation-state. Similarly, Kretsedemas and Brotherton (2008) have detailed the many ways in which immigration is policed and regulated by multiple agencies within the nation-state, during both pro- and anti-immigration periods. There has been considerable interest in the historical use of immigration enforcement to regulate labour flows (see Calavita, 2008). More recently, the use of immigration enforcement in relation to moral panics around crime, terrorism and racial tensions, which Kretsedemas and Brotherton (2008) suggest are expressions of an identifiably global anti-immigration sentiment. The most significant contribution of this literature has been the exploration of the refugee, asylum seeker or extra legal migrant as both subject and object of criminalisation and exclusion (see Young, 2007; Melossi, 2003; Calavita, 2003; Green & Grewcock, 2002). This work has important implications for the present study and is worthy of considered reflection. In the first instance, it has been claimed that in many countries of the Global North immigration enforcement has become one of the fastest growing areas of law enforcement spending (Kretsedemas & Brotherton, 2008; Pickering, 2004), and that those apprehended are becoming a growing proportion of incarcerated populations against whom deportation is increasingly being used as a key strategy of crime control. In the second instance, this body of work retrains our focus onto the legal and administrative systems and practices which are constantly determining and redetermining how a non-citizen is to be regarded as legal, illegal or somewhere in between.

The significance of borders, however, is relatively new to criminology (Pickering & Weber, 2006). Borders have historically been taken for granted in criminological inquiry because the study of crime and deviance has largely been demarcated by the criminal law and/or criminal activity (or lack thereof) within a jurisdiction. Jurisdictions have largely, albeit not exclusively, mapped onto the territorial nation-state. Therefore, traditional criminology has been defined by a jurisdictional limitation that has also been a territorial limitation. This is not to suggest that anti-immigration sentiment (Cole, 2008) and the policing of the alien "Other" are recent phenomena (Finnane, 2009). Rather, sustained criminological attention has not traditionally been focused on the broader importance of the border in seeking understandings of crime and crime control.

However, as the border has increasingly become a site for the performance of security, notably through the policing of the movement of people under conditions of globalisation, its significance has also been increasingly questioned. The border has spawned two criminological approaches. The first has adopted a state-centric approach which broadly views the nation-state and its territorial borders as fixed, and hence the policing that occurs in defence of those borders as similarly anchored to an immutable aspect of nationhood. In many ways, this literature has been informed by security studies and the growing alignment of criminology with broader national security concerns. The second has problematised the fixed nature of the state, and contends that the territorial sovereign state is continually being reproduced by often-changing performances of border security, and that those involved in the political performance of policing and those impacted by it are in constant negotiation and struggle over the meaning and implications of border policing. The normalising force of borders (Soguk, 1999), and the focus upon them as important sites for securitisation and crime control, has been challenged by criminological incursions that have sought to highlight the ways in which borders can become sites for the commission of a range of significant harms. The border as a site of securitisation and crime control has given rise to important critical criminological inquiry into the nature and impact of harm that border enforcement generates. Grewcock (2010), Green (2006), Green and Grewcock (2002), Michalowski (2007), Wonders (2006) and Pickering (2005) have identified the border and its protection as a significant site of state criminality and organised deviance. This scholarship has also pointed to the malleability of borders for expansionist criminal justice control, and the trialling and instalment of pre-emptive and pre-crime strategies (see McCulloch & Pickering, 2009). Grounded in this second approach, this book is an attempt to read gender into a criminology of the border.

Women's experiences of border policing have been the focus of few studies. The greatest attention has been given to sexual violence along fortified border regions, most notably the US–Mexico border. For example, the policing of borders has been considered a site for the exclusionary policing of sexuality, which in turn has fundamentally shaped US migration control strategies (Luibheid, 2005). Luibheid's study of sexual violence inflicted by border patrol officials on the US–Mexico border revealed cultures of impunity in relation to violence against women. Carpenter (2006) has similarly argued that the militarisation of the US–Mexico border has created a more hostile and violent environment for women. Her focus on the use of rape at the border builds on Falcon's (2001, cited in Carpenter 2006) earlier work in which she concluded that rapes along the border have been systematic and racialised in two main ways: rape as a form of national security and rape as a mechanism of warfare. Falcon argues that both forms are institutionalised and have come about because of the ideological dominance of national security cast as a military problem with military solutions and administered through a masculinist policy elite and male-dominated enforcement apparatus.

The post-9/11 escalation of border securitisation has been part of the "global crackdown" on illegal immigration, which in turn has made asylum a more pressing constraint on sovereignty than ever before (Dauvergne, 2008). Understanding the ways in which this plays out for women is considered in Chap. 4. The securitisation of borders that has increasingly emerged since September 11 has also intensified the growth of the market for irregular migration, with concomitant increases in vulnerability and exposure to violence, especially for women (Kapur, 2002). As Kyle and Koslowski's (2001) seminal work has demonstrated, border enforcement and smuggling operations exist in a symbiotic relationship. In this book I am interested in how gender can shape this symbiotic relationship, and the many ways in which smuggling manifests, including as a highly nebulous and complicated process of facilitated movement.

Chapter 5 considers women's extra legal border crossing in relation to sex trafficking. It argues that much of the policing that seeks to stop trafficking is actually played out through at best regulation and at worst criminalisation of women legitimately working in the sex industry. Moreover, the extraordinary focus on sex trafficking diminishes the harms perpetrated in other forms of labour exploitation and trafficking.

7   Women at the Border

With the increasing focus on borders and securitisation criminologists have become more alert to the impact of the expanding policing apparatus which is deployed in highly racialised and gendered ways. Yet women's experience of crossing borders is far more complex than coming face-to-face with border policing agents. The research referenced in this book suggests that women's extra legal crossing of borders is shaped by the informal policing and criminality of both state and non-state agents, and by restrictions on their mobility occurring during flight from their country of origin, while in transit, as well as after their arrival. The fortification of borders is far more complex than the militarisation of the enforcement of a specific geographical border, and the experience of enforcement is far more complicated than dealing with individual or collectives of state agents.

The challenge addressed in this book is to consider this broadening of actors and contexts for the commissions of crime and harm in border and frontier zones through which women transit, and indeed live, for often extended periods. Women's extra legal mobility is rarely linear (cf. Sassen), and is often delayed in parts. There-fore, this book is also a consideration of how we might understand mobility to better grapple with the parameters and dynamism of crime and harm that surround extra legal border crossing.

In previous work I undertook with Weber (2006), we argued that global mobility is increasingly becoming a basis for the stratification of the world's populations and that criminalisation plays a key role in this process. This book presents the argument that processes of criminalisation are only one part, albeit an important part, of this stratification. In addition, we need to be attentive to the ways in which crime and violence, radiating out from the border and enacted by a range of agents, also play defining roles in the organisation and reorganisation of mobility and the fundamentally racial and gendered determinants of these processes.

Available figures evidence women crossing borders extra legally less frequently than men. Indeed, it is often accepted that the character of illegal cross-border mobility has been inherently male. This has been explained with reference to many factors, including the difficulties women face in overcoming social and legal re-strictions on their movement when seeking to escape or depart from a place. It has been noted by some that women's mobility has been restricted because of their lack of social networks, which many male migrants often rely in transit and destination countries (see Koser & Pinkerton, 2002). However, there is some evidence to sug-gest that women are increasingly undertaking extra legal border crossings regard-less. Chapter 2 examines this in relation to the movement of women from Africa through Malta and into Europe. There is also evidence to suggest that key border crossing points are becoming more dangerous.

The overall aim of this book is to illustrate how women's extra legal border crossing necessitates a study of the border that goes far beyond the territorial border. This book explores how conflict produces forms of gender violence that constitute both deterrents and catalysts to mobility, as well as forms of enforcement and polic-ing of women's mobility.

In this book I am concerned with understanding women's experiences of extra legal border crossing and exploring these based upon the following three premises:

1. Extra legal border crossing occurs in the context of unchecked violence.
2. Border policing occurs beyond and within territorial borders and is enacted by state and non-state agents.

3. Border crossing neither begins nor ends with the extra legal border crossing of a national territorial border.

Migrations do not simply happen—they are produced (Sassen, 1998, 1999). Equally, the border, and how we enforce it, is produced. Many national borders are a product of colonialism and hence women's mobility is policed not only at national borders but also at the remnants of internal borders that retain inflections of territory and the markers of which are historically grounded in social, legal and political relations and structures. This book is focused on the thick descriptions of women's extra legal border crossings. The outcome is a decentring of the state and of formal border policing initiatives, and the descriptions work to train our attention onto the complex contexts in which women negotiate extra legal border crossing.

8   Summary

Women's extra legal border crossing is a growing phenomenon. However, our understanding is limited by the poor quality and availability of reliable data on women's mobility. There is no reliable scholarly study on global trends in women's extra legal movement, or of the nature and scope of their extra legal border crossings. This chapter considers the debates around women and global mobility along with analysis of studies of violence against women. It develops a framework for understanding women's experiences of being policed out of the Global North through a range of state and non-state measures.

Chapter 2
The Journey to the Border: Continuums of Crossing

1 Introduction

The focus of this chapter is the impact of violence on women's capacity to cross national borders. The aim is to better understand crime, violence and mobility in relation to women fleeing what many regard as a collapsed state and site of one of the world's most intractable conflicts: Somalia. We approach this subject by considering women's experiences of conflict and the conditions surrounding their *exit,* their *transit* through refugee camps and/or neighbouring countries, and their *reception* in countries of asylum or the Global North. We argue that an increase in the number of women fleeing conflict zones such as Somalia is occurring at the same time that extra legal border crossing is becoming increasingly difficult and dangerous. We also argue that the conditions of exit, transit and reception are shaped by both organised and opportunistic crime. Green and Ward (2009) have recently termed crime that serves both organised and opportunistic goals as "dual purpose" criminality. Ordinary, political or indeed dual purpose criminality effectively acts as a border policing apparatus that controls women's mobility, thus gatekeeping women's access to other countries, and in many cases access to legal remedies and protection. Such criminality can be enacted by organised political groups, militia, individuals or groups from opposing clans, government agents, smugglers and traffickers, or can take the form of the structural violence entailed in reception processes in places like Malta. Such criminality largely controls the nature of the border crossing experience for women fleeing Somalia. Furthermore, this criminality may be regarded as a form of political, cultural, organised and individualised policing of women's mobility that routinely employs practices of rape and sexual violence.

This chapter charts the experience of women crossing borders extra legally, fleeing conflict in Somalia and arriving in Malta. Malta has been at the forefront of regional Europe's efforts to reshape itself in order to prevent and counter global mobility. This research was originally focused on women's experiences of extra legal

---

This chapter was co-authored with Alison Gerard, Monash University.

S. Pickering, *Women, Borders, and Violence,*
DOI 10.1007/978-1-4419-0271-9_2, © Springer Science+Business Media, LLC 2011

crossing into Malta. By nationality Somali women are currently the largest group of women arriving in Malta (National Statistics Office, 2009). Their extra legal border crossing of the Mediterranean, often from Libya into Malta, is the final in a series of extra legal border crossings from Somalia to Malta. Consequently, this chapter begins with an exploration of women's experiences of mobility and border crossing within Somalia, including moving across Somali territory controlled by different militia and clans, across the borders with Somalia's immediate neighbours—Kenya and the refugee camps inside the Kenyan border—and then the border crossing experience through transit countries such as Libya and Sudan, immediately prior to attempts to enter Europe via Malta. It then considers women's experiences of violence upon arrival and extended detention and confinement in Malta.

There is an inherent difficulty in systematically obtaining information about women's extra legal border crossings using traditional data sources which overwhelmingly fail to record gender let alone the impact that gender has on unauthorised migration and attempts to police it at the border. For example, Malta does not systematically disaggregate refugee data by gender. Research on Somalia has been limited to the testimony of women who have reached Malta along with secondary material drawn from the limited scholarship and human rights reports on the country. Physical insecurity and limited accessibility have militated against field-based research in Somalia (Hagmann, 2005; Crisp 2000, 2004). Somalia has been considered too hostile for international actors to maintain ongoing operations. In 2005, UN and UA troops withdrew because they considered the casualties too great. International non-government organisations, UNHCR and others who routinely work in contexts of protracted conflict have repeatedly withdrawn from Somalia. Indeed, only one international non-government organisation has maintained a constant presence in Somalia since 1991 (Noor, 2007). The conflict has meant that any meaningful collection of data on the level and nature of violence, or on the numbers of deaths, rapes and forced migrations are at best estimates, and the usual methodological limitations of such counts in conflict situations are compounded by concerns over physical security and access to affected populations. Attributing moral let alone legal responsibility to crime in Somalia is as difficult as it might be useful or meaningful. By comparison, violence in Somalia may be considered as occurring on such a scale that it can easily daunt any meaningful criminological analysis, and instead intellectual analysis is left to the scholars of international relations or those concerned with the political economy of war (cf. Menkhaus, 2004). At the very point at which violence cannot be meaningfully understood as crime and only meaningfully understood as war, women's accounts of attempting to flee Somalia, and cross borders to gain protection, suggest that experiences of rape evidence some pattern of criminality that achieves both opportunistic and more organised goals. As Green and Ward (2009, p. 609) argue: "…there is no simple distinction between, on the one hand, violence serving the organisational goals either of state or non-state political actors and, on the other, violence for individual gratification. The same violent act often serves both purposes". The impact of this violence in Somalia on women has fundamentally shaped their experience of crossing borders to escape the conflict.

2   Violence, Rape and Criminality in Conflict

Nowhere has a state collapse been so profound, prolonged or misunderstood as in Somalia (Menkhaus, 2004). Somalia has had no effective government since 1991 when the government of Siyad Barre was overthrown after 16 years in power. What sets Somalia apart from other failed states is that it has not been able to maintain even a weak central government or a modicum of juridical sovereignty (Menkhaus, 2004). As Menkhaus has described, "Somalia is a failure among failed states" (2004, p. 17).

The United Nations intervened in Somalia in 1993 (UNOSOM), only to withdraw in 1995. The unrelenting violence perpetrated by militia, those that have attempted government, neighbouring countries, international actors and criminal actors is complex and cannot be covered in a single chapter (see Lewis, 2002; Bestemen, 1996). Increasingly subject to criticism, the limited scholarship on Somalia has often problematically reduced conflict in the country to "anarchy" and "lawlessness" and has been rooted in cultural essentialisms (see Beestemen, 1996 for a detailed critique of stereotypes of Somalia). According to such analyses, "...the civil war and state collapse transformed Somali politics into senseless infighting between clan factions, everyday life consisted of marauding militia intoxicated by *khat*, and the absence of a central government threatened regional stability and the effectiveness of the international community" (Hagmann, 2005, p. 526). On this account, Somalia was to be viewed as an aberration that exemplified "development in reverse" (Lindley, 2009, p. 33). However, a nascent critical scholarship on Somalia is evidencing more complex analyses of the power relationships and networks of control that have developed since the 1990s and intensified over the past few years in the most recent phase of the conflict. Instead of reducing violence and insecurity (along with all of the other factors that contribute to the parlous state of health, education and governance in Somalia) to the status of a "failed state", this recent scholarship suggests the benefits of decentring a statist conception of violence. For example, the *Human Development Report* for Somalia in 2001 (Bradbury, Menkhaus, & Marchal, 2001) understood the collapse of the Somali state as a process rather than an event, noting that the measures of development did not significantly alter with the outbreak of civil war in the early 1990s. Rather, the Report argues, the provision of services, the rise of black markets and the increased importance of kinship could all be evidenced prior to 1991. Indeed, "state collapse and warfare were most effective in achieving what structural adjustments had failed to bring about: the total privatisation of all public services from water to electricity, and schooling to security.... Highly dependent on remittances from its worldwide diaspora, Somalia gradually evolved into an entrepot economy and a labour reserve for the global market" (Hagmann, 2005, p. 528).

Hagmann has argued that the absence of government should not be considered to be synonymous with the absence of governance in Somalia or the predominance of conflict and criminality. However, there is agreement that the conflict can be regarded as rooted in intense ethnic and communal antagonisms and high levels of organised violence and deliberate targeting of individuals: "...the fighting has been sustained by the fact that various actors—politicians, warlords, militia groups, local entrepreneurs and international business concerns—have a vested economic interest in the continuation of armed conflict" (Crisp, 2003). Menkhaus similarly argues that the collapse of central government is not inherently linked to criminality, and instead advances a taxonomy that understands the collapse of the state through three interdependent crises: (1) the protracted collapse of central government, (2) protracted armed conflict and (3) lawlessness. It is by exploring the intersection of ethnic and communal antagonisms, organised violence and individual targeting that this chapter considers women's experience of violence in fleeing Somalia.

Menkhaus (2004) refers to Somalia as a case of protracted state collapse and the theatre for a proxy war between Ethiopia and its Arab rivals:

> Arab states seek a strong central Somali state to counterbalance and outflank Ethiopia; Ethiopia seeks a weak, decentralised client state, and is willing to settle for ongoing state collapse rather than risk a revived Arab-backed government in Mogadishu. Both have provided military and financial support to their Somali clients, reinforcing the tendency towards violent political stalemate. (Menkhaus, 2004, p. 9)

If we accept Hagmann's argument that the collapse of the state and the ongoing conflict have "catalysed" Somalia's modernisation then we need to consider how violence against women, and specifically of the practice of rape, has been shaped by the contested local authorities that are often in varying states of flux, and the associated free market capitalism based on largely unfettered entrepreneurship that continues to make use of historically, culturally and religiously based social control processes in Somalia. This chapter therefore focuses on how we might make (criminological) sense of the sexual violence women experience when they cross borders in order to gain protection. Criminology has long been concerned with crimes against the person, even if it has been less concerned with collapsed states such as Somalia. This chapter explores the relationship between organised crime, opportunistic crime (which we argue has been carried out by organised groups, or what may be understood as the conflict entrepreneurs of Somalia) and the individuals who enact a dual purpose criminality against women fleeing Somalia.

There has been some debate about the nature of lawlessness and criminality in Somalia. Conditions immediately following the collapse of the state have been perceived as conducive to opportunistic crime not dissimilar to what has occurred in other conflict zones following an invasion or toppling of a regime. Menkhaus argues that there is evidence of Somali communities establishing and maintaining high levels of lawful behaviour and personal security either through clan customary law, the enforcement of blood payments for wrongs committed or the application of customary law (p. 31). The effectiveness of these systems is dependent on the relationships between local clans. From his observations, while such systems are subject to rapid and substantial change, they form a social order in which "[w]holesale looting, rape and murder associated with armed clashes rarely occur" (2004, p. 32). Instead, violent crime is more likely to be addressed via the related informal systems of customary law and blood payments. This occurs in the absence of formal law enforcement, which effectively collapsed with the state. However,

Menkhaus' conclusion is based on two unaddressed assumptions: that all members of communities are equally protected by such forms of social control and justice; and that the forms of violent behaviour noted as being rare are not themselves being transformed and committed in changing contexts. However, our research, together with that of human rights organisations, supports the finding of Menkhaus that the most devastating forms of criminality are committed by political leaders and business groupings. In supporting his analysis, Menkhaus cites the types of kidnapping which draw together various alliances between gangs and business and political interests in enforcing the control of territory and resources. Our research similarly suggests that criminality and violence result from problematic alliances between opportunists and organised interests, yet we also find that such violence can be traced in their practice of rape and sexual violence.

The situation in Somalia has been misunderstood because Somalia has undergone significant changes since 1991, yet most analyses have remained static (Menkhaus, 2004). For the purposes of this chapter, we need to be mindful of how criminality against women has changed since 1991 without recourse to pathologisation or assumptions regarding the nature or causes of violence. Prior to 9/11 collapsed states were considered a threat to international peace and security in political rather than strategic terms and only partially attracted a meaningful response from the international community. The rape of Somali women captured international attention in the early 1990s; however, international focus shifted to conflicts in Rwanda and the former Yugoslavia where rape was recognised as a war crime and form of ethnic cleansing. According to human rights reports, since the early 1990s rape and sexual violence in Somalia have often, albeit not exclusively, been committed by groups of men. The impact of this violence is shaped not only by the fact that the victims are women, but also by their imputed ethnicity or other identity markers. More recent research concurs with the view that rape often results in communal ostracism of the victim and even punishment for being the victim of the crime and thus offending familial or communal honour (Musse, 2004; HRW, 2009c). To this end, the discussion in this chapter shares some of the elements of the assertions of Green and Ward (2009) in their consideration of sexual violence in post-invasion Iraq. In the case of Somalia an additional issue must be considered: that of the currency of rape in purchasing women's and men's mobility out of Somalia. Rape is not only a form of violent ritual (cf. Tilly, 2003) but also a transaction for travel whereby women, as targets of rape, become the currency of exchange for both men and women seeking to exit Somalia. Women are targets for rape because of the gendered, cultural and communal consequences of having been raped.

The conflict and collapse of the state in Somalia have left women particularly vulnerable.[1] Yet at the same time gender roles in Somalia have changed since the beginning of the civil war—some have even suggested that gender roles have been

---

[1] Despite the high levels of gender-based violence in Somalia, it is important to recognise the many examples of women's resistance to violence and conflict. While not the focus of this chapter, other authors have cogently made this argument: see, for example, the collection by Gardner and El Bushra (2004).

"reversed" (Hagmann, 2005). Gardner and El Bushra (2004) documented the impact of the conflict on women's roles in relation to both displacement and the division of labour. They evidence that displacement has increasingly meant women have become the main breadwinners and that international efforts at increasing women's political involvement have also led to their increasing participation in reconciliation activities. Gardner and El Bushra's edited collection further evidences the ways in which women are increasingly negotiating multiple clans—those of both their husband and their maternal family. Straddling two clans has resulted in clear benefits for displaced families when women have had to deal with travelling through territory controlled by other clans. However, crimes against women have marked women's efforts at negotiating any new individual or collective status.

3   Part 1: Fleeing Conflict, Crossing Borders

The capacity and opportunity to exit a country is a precondition for being able to access another. Many women who have crossed borders extra legally must first negotiate, confront and escape the conditions of exit from their home country. As the analysis above suggests, a range of actors are often involved in both the formal and informal means of preventing them from fleeing. From our research it is clear that rape is a central consequence for women fleeing violence in Somalia.

3.1   Fleeing Somalia

3.1.1   Rape on the Road

Most recently those who have fled Somalia by sea have often used the Gulf of Aden to reach Yemen. This dangerous sea voyage is almost exclusively controlled by people smugglers operating out of the lawless region of Puntland. UNHCR suggests that capsizing and drowning are commonplace. In one eight-month period in 2008, 261 Somalis died attempting this crossing. Because the passage is controlled by smugglers, additional anti-apprehension strategies have further endangered lives—for example, UNHCR has documented cases of smugglers forcing refugees off boats and into the sea to avoid apprehension. For women on board boats sexual violence is a constant threat. Reports indicate that rape and sexual harassment are routine during these already dangerous crossings (HRW, 2009c). Women who have arrived on Yemeni beaches have reported being raped trying to make their way from the landing point to a safe place. "The victims of these abuses know they cannot complain to the authorities without risking arrest, and the people who target them are well aware of that as well" (HRW, 2009c, p. 3).

In the early 1990s, at the outbreak of the civil war in Somalia, the most typical route for those fleeing the violence was to walk to the border with north-eastern

Kenya in small groups, making the dangerous voyage by boat to Kenya's shores. The threat of violence, especially rape, for women taking the land route has been documented by non-government organisations. The experience of a young Somali woman walking along the road south towards the Kenyan border was recently documented by Human Rights Watch:

> Militiamen waylaid our car. They stopped our driver forcefully by use of gunshots and threatened to kill him if he did not stop. He complied. They ransacked all of the passengers. There were only three [young] women out of the fourteen on board—the rest were all children and older people. All three of us were raped. They took us to some bushes near the highway. The militiamen were five in number. Two kept watch and forced the driver not to go anywhere, while three of the butchers took us to a nearby thicket and raped us. Each of them went for one of us. I did not suffer too much bodily harm other than kicks and blows and slaps. I gave in because I heard stories of girls who tried to resist being frightened by having bullets shot between their legs or by other ways. From there we were brought back to the car. They took our personal belongings and disappeared into the bush. (HRW, 2008, p. 82)

Those fleeing Mogadishu often take the road to Afgooye just outside the capital, along which temporary IDP settlements have been built. Those fleeing have been described as finding "…that the brutality they fled has followed them there. And those who choose to risk travelling further to seek asylum abroad must run a deadly gauntlet of abusive freelance militias, soldiers, police, and human smugglers" (HRW, 2008). The NGOs that have operated inside Somalia have documented that the act of travelling and attempting to cross borders entails an enormous risk of violence. "Human Rights Watch interviewed refugees who were raped, robbed, beaten, imprisoned, or tortured while trying to reach the country's borders. Some saw their travelling companions murdered on the road" (HRW, 2008). Militias operate along the main roads and stop vehicles transporting refugees. Women recount stories of being stopped and raped by such groups, or watching other women be raped. Many women described how they or other women travelling in their group could be held for up to weeks at a time and repeatedly raped at various points along the border, effectively paying a "toll" for their vehicle to pass through militia-held territory.

3.2   Transit: Libya

Libya is usually the last African point on the journey to Europe for many women from the Horn of Africa. Most migrants and refugees arriving in Italy have set sail from the Libyan coast. The overwhelming majority of refugees intercepted by Maltese authorities to date have boarded in Libya (NSO, 2009). Those who make the crossing rely on people smugglers. The crossing from Malta is particularly dangerous. In 2008, 2,100 people and in 2007, 1,900 people died attempting to make this crossing (USCRI, 2009). Since 2008, NGOs have been documenting the refusal of Libyan authorities to go to the aid of vessels in distress. In 2009 Libya entered into an agreement with the Italian Government for the Italian navy to patrol the Libyan coast. Under this arrangement Libyan personnel on board are charged with interdicting migrants. In May 2009, the Italian navy transferred a group of refugees picked up off the coast of Malta back to Tripoli after an agreement had been struck between the two governments. This followed the signing of a "Treaty of Friendship, Partnership and Co-operation" between Libya and Italy, which included the joint patrol of the sea. The Treaty, which focused on financially compensating Libya for Italy's occupation, included Libya agreeing to increase its control of its territorial and international waters and to accept refugees interdicted at sea attempting to enter Italy. Moreover, Libya has agreed to tighten security of its southern borders in response to increased extra legal border crossings. This effectively a "contracts out" of Italy's refugee obligations to a country that is not a signatory to the Refugee Convention.

Libya is considered to have relatively high living standards and good employment opportunities, and those seeking to enter Europe have reported transiting for months or even years in Libya, working both in the formal and informal economies to fund the price of their voyage to Europe. Women who had worked in Libya to fund their travel to Malta report that it was easier for women than men to gain work in the informal economies, often in cleaning, domestic service and related activities. Refugees in Libya have no right to work and limited health care is provided through UNHCR.

Their lack of social status in Libya also makes women vulnerable, both at work and in public spaces. Women report being fearful of violence because they believed the authorities would not protect them or respond to crimes against them, as well as fearing the violence of the authorities who had the power to deport them.

There have been reports of women being held in houses run by authorities and having to pay them a required sum of money to be allowed to leave—if they could not pay they were raped. Women are reluctant to share first-person experiences of these houses, but clearly many knew in detail the activities conducted within them. Smugglers have used sexual violence against refugees both as "payment" for their services and opportunistically. Smugglers have been operating with virtual impunity and sometimes in concert with the authorities in Libya. A recent report found:

> The traffickers were involved with the soldiers. They work with the government to keep the special house outside Tripoli. There were 32 of us held in this house, 25 men and 7 women. They didn't respect the women. They saw one girl and admired her. They forced her into a room. She said to me three times, "Why didn't you save me?" I answered, "What could I do?" She said, "They forced me." I cried. I couldn't do anything. (HRW, 2009c)

For the past five years, human rights organisations have documented Libya's forced return of refugees. Most recently, this has included the Libyan Government threatening to summarily deport an estimated one million foreigners without legal status (USCRI, 2009).

UNHCR has seen a steady increase in the number of asylum seekers in Libya, from 676 in 2005 to 2256 in the first six months of 2009. It has been alleged that the Libyan Government and law enforcement agencies are involved in people smuggling. Research has found that "One Somali asylum seeker said he went to the Somali Embassy to pay his money for the boat trip and was transported directly from the embassy to the point of departure" (HRW, 2009c). Human rights organisations have also detailed evidence of "smugglers houses" (HRW, 2009c). For example, Human Rights Watch found in a recent report:

> …both men and women told Human Rights Watch that they frequently saw smugglers and police separate or try to separate women from groups of migrants. They told Human Rights Watch that they believed the women were being taken away to be sexually assaulted. In addition to sexual abuse, women interviewed by Human Rights Watch also described other violations, including beatings, lack of adequate sanitation, and extortion. Sexual abuse may occur—not only at the hands of smugglers but also for women migrants in police custody. (HRW, 2009c)

In an interview for the Human Rights Watch report researchers were told:

> The smugglers used police handcuffs, so we thought they were with the police, but they did not wear police uniforms. They handcuffed two or three people to frighten us. The smuggler used to say, "I'll kill you if you do not pay the money." He also said, "I will take you to prison." I paid the $800. He handed us to another smuggler who took us to Ajdabiya, where we were held for one month and where they again held us for ransom and demanded more money. The beatings there were even more severe because we couldn't pay the money.

In another interview they were told:

> They took us to a big house that held a lot of Eritreans and Somalis, about 190 people. The doors were locked. We couldn't go out. We spent one week in that room. Every day, the Libyans came and took women to do whatever they wanted with them. No one slept well. We were worried that they would turn us over to the police. No one had the right to ask any questions.

3.2.1   Rape in the Camps

The available data indicate that most women fleeing Somalia travel via Yemen where they are able to obtain prima facie refugee status. However, as previously noted the voyage is hazardous and women's vulnerability to sexual violence en route and upon arrival is significant (HRW, 2009c). Another main route taken is via Kenya, which has ordinarily resulted in extended, if not indefinite, periods in refugee camps, which is discussed further below.

Somali refugees who reached the Kenyan border could register with UNHCR, which effectively protected them from immediate deportation were they apprehended by Kenyan authorities. In early 2007, the border between Kenya and Somalia was closed and is now patrolled by Kenyan police charged with keeping out Somali refugees. This means that refugees need to make an unauthorised and dangerous desert crossing. This crossing is increasingly undertaken at night, and increasingly involves the use of smugglers to avoid being apprehended by Kenyan police. Non-government organisations have documented the use of bribes to pay Kenyan police to be released, with those who could not afford this being immediately deported to Somalia (HRW, 2009c). The border was closed in response to US concerns that this route could be used by terrorists moving between Somalia and Kenya, hence endangering Kenyan national security. On the day the border was closed, 420 Somalis were deported, the vast majority of whom were women (Amnesty International,

2007). The border between Kenya and Somalia is almost 700 km long, and despite the fortification and patrol efforts since the border was closed, refugees continue to cross, running the gauntlet between the border and one of the refugee camps they need to reach in order to register with UNHCR and avoid deportation. The closure of the border has resulted in increasing corrupt or criminal activity of Kenyan police, including bribes, violence and rape (HRW, 2009a): "Kenya's police now have free reign to intercept and demand bribes from Somali refugees attempting to reach Dadaab's camps, threatening deportation and inflicting violence if refugees refuse" (HRW, 2009a, p. 21). It has been reported that women apprehended by police are at risk of being raped both in the outdoors but also within police stations. Historically, Kenya has been reluctant to host refugees from Somalia, citing concerns over their impact on national security. However, Kenya has more recently been admitting refugees because of its obligations under the Organisation for African Unity, and because to do otherwise might be perceived by important international aid donors and others as undermining efforts at promoting democracy and broader human rights standards. However, the events of 9/11 and US pressure provided the rationale and resources to close the border and stop the flow of refugees. The Kenya–Somalia border has emerged as a strategic interest for the United States. Recent research indicates that such efforts have not effectively sealed the border, but rather have entrenched a hostile space in which rape and corruption are perpetrated.

Kenyan refugee camps are overcrowded and made up predominantly of women and children, the elderly and other vulnerable groups who are poor and getting poorer (Crisp, 2004). Militia operate within and around the camps. Kenyan refugee camps are almost entirely reliant on international aid. They are home to "angry young men" (Turner, 1999) confronted by the collective realignment of gender relations and UNHCR and international aid groups effectively usurping the historically unquestioned patriarchal rule. Despite efforts at various informal and formal legal and policing responses to violence in the camps, most recent reports indicate that there is an absence of effective legal, political or sexual protection in the camps (Pittaway & Bartolemei, 2004).

Refugee camps contain a concentration of violence based on conditions of pervasive insecurity, the quantification of which is almost impossible to manage (Crisp, 2000). Refugees face ongoing insecurity in the two main refugee camps in Kenya: Kakuma and Dadaab. Crisp's (2000) typology of violence in Kenyan refugee camps includes: domestic and community violence; sexual abuse and sexual violence; armed robbery and violence both within and between national refugee groups. This typology demonstrates the significant burden of violence that women experience in these camps. Customary systems of justice in operation in the camps, either with the actual or tacit approval of UNHCR, the Kenyan Government and other international aid agencies, routinely rely on forcing victims of rape to marry their attackers, or if the victim has been attacked by a member of another clan her male relatives may receive compensation which she cannot access (Crisp, 2000). Numerous scholarly and NGO reports highlight that refugee women have experienced rape and other forms of gender-based violence in the camps since their inception. This research has paralleled work that has historically recognised the prevalence of rape and sexual violence as a routine part of the refugee experience (Pittaway & Bartolemei, 2004; Crisp, 2000, 2004). While international and grassroots organisations have worked to reduce the incidence of sexual violence in camps there are inherent problems with data collection on the incidence of sexual violence as well as service delivery to the survivors of attacks. There has also been some debate regarding the extent to which agencies such as UNHCR should bear the responsibility (let alone whether they have the resources) to ensure the physical safety and security of refugees in the camps (Crisp, 2000).

At the outbreak of conflict in 1991 UNHCR was alerted to the seemingly high level of rape in the Kenyan refugee camps. In a seven-month study (February–August 1993) UNHCR documented 192 cases of rape in these camps, including four against children and one against a man. Of these, 85 were reported to have occurred inside Somalia while the remaining 107 occurred inside the Kenyan refugee camps. UNHCR noted that these were the reported cases and expected the real figure to be approximately ten times higher.

> In an overwhelming number of cases, refugee women and girls are violently attacked by unknown armed bandits at night or when they go to the outskirts of the refugee camp to herd goats or collect firewood. According to UNHCR, nearly all (100 of the 107) rape cases that occurred in the Kenyan camps were committed by bandits. Increasingly, these bandits join forces with former Somali military men or fighters from the various warring factions who launch raids across the Kenya–Somali border. To a lesser extent, refugee women are also vulnerable to attack by Kenyan police officers posted in the area, who were responsible for seven reported rape cases. (HRW, 1993, p. 1)

There is general agreement in the extant literature that the perpetrators of rape and sexual violence in the camps include local Kenyans, Somali refugees, Somali militia involved in cross-border activity, Kenyan border police and military personnel. Reports indicate that most attacks involve more than one perpetrator (Musse, 2004), and that the same perpetrators are involved in the commission of armed robberies at night and perpetrate the rapes by day (Crisp, 2000). Refugee scholars have often analysed violence in the camps, including the use of rape, as opportunistic—"There are simply more items to steal, more people to rob and more women to rape in and around the camps that [sic] in other parts of the two provinces" (Crisp, 2000, p. 619)—or as a "weapon of war" (Fitzgerald, 1998) used by one clan against another.

However, rape and sexual violence against women cannot be understood only by recourse to opportunistic explanations of criminal activity. From the available studies of rape in the refugee camps, it is evident that over half of the women raped knew their attackers, and almost all were gang raped (Musse, 2004). Victims of rape were effectively "chosen" because of their clan affiliation: "Many women said that the rapists would ask their clan affiliation or demand to know the location of dwellings of a particular clan. The attackers would then target the women of that group. Women who were from the same clan as their attackers were often spared from being raped and were only robbed" (Musse, 2004, p. 73). Clan affiliation was integral to transforming the rape from an "opportunistic" crime to an act intended to extract political effect. The cultural stigma of rape has long-term political and social ramifications for the women attacked, their families and their clans. These consequences can differ for women of different marital, social and cultural backgrounds. The possible outcomes for women who are raped include rejection by their families (and consequent exclusion from economic and other protections as well as social and cultural isolation), and for an unmarried woman removal of her chances of making a successful marriage. Rape brings shame and stigma to the families involved, members of which may also be ostracised. Most importantly, however, the rape of a woman by an attacker from a rival clan symbolises their dominance and defilement of the victim's clan, which is accomplished by the possibility of the woman then bearing the child of a member of the opposing clan.

4   Part 2: Reception: Malta

It is estimated that the sea journey from Africa to Malta takes between two and five days. Boats set sail from either Libya or Tunisia (Ostergaard, 2008). It is common for it to take more than one attempt to successfully reach Malta or another European port.

Government officials and NGOs agree that there has been a significant recent increase in the number of single women arriving from sub-Saharan Africa, including Somalia. There is also some consensus as to women's reasons for fleeing: some leave for economic reasons, some because of gender-based persecution, and some for more general protection needs. Experiences vary significantly across the female asylum seeker population and are dependent on whether women travel alone, have access to social capital, travel with men and children, or whether they are pregnant. Regardless, conditions are difficult for women when they arrive in Malta and while they await refugee determination. Access to paid work is only possible once they are released from the detention centres, and discrimination often prevents them from gaining employment. There are reports of women being forced into prostitution or ending up in prostitution after they arrive. Prostitution is sometimes carried out in transit or en route to Malta, either coercively or as a way to fund the voyage. Many of the women arriving in Malta have experienced rape or other sexual violence in Somalia en route, in transit in Libya, or throughout all parts of their journey. Some make the journey from Somalia to Malta relatively quickly because they have family and clan-based connections which assist them. Others have to stay in Libya to raise money, while others escape prostitution by coming to Malta. Women are reluctant to discuss their knowledge and experience of prostitution, whether coerced or not, because of the associated shame and stigma. The violence experienced throughout the previous stages of fleeing Somalia does not simply cease once in Malta, but rather is perpetrated in a different context: within the European system of warehousing asylum seekers in Malta, of which the proportion of women is significantly increasing (NSO, 2009).

Over the last decade—Malta, a European Union member state since 2004—has rapidly become a country on the frontline of policing irregular migration. Geographically positioned on Europe's southern border, Malta is receiving growing numbers of people arriving by boat who are seeking asylum. The majority of people arriving commenced their long and treacherous journeys in Horn of Africa and West African countries (NSO, 2009, p. 3). The response of the Maltese Government to extra legal border crossing has been hostile and punitive, and in spite of efforts to put in place appropriate refugee determination processes has faced international condemnation for its use of detention. *Médicins Sans Frontières* classes its treatment of refugees as inhuman (2009, p. 1), particularly for its impact on vulnerable populations including single women and pregnant women, and for the historical practice of not separating women from detained male populations.

In stark disproportion to its tiny land mass, Malta's maritime boundaries award it a search and rescue area that stretches for some 250,000 km^2 (Lutterbeck, 2009, p. 128), or 790 times its land mass. This has placed considerable strain on Malta's maritime squadron in the context of policing unauthorised arrivals. Two thirds of all arrivals in Malta are rescue operations (Communication with government official). The Armed Forces of Malta (AFM) has responsibility for the significant search and rescue area around Malta. Malta has an economic interest in sustaining this broad zone as the country receives revenues from air traffic that earn the government approximately 8 million € per year (Lutterbeck, 2009, p. 133). Approximately half of the boats are intercepted by the AFM prior to reaching Maltese shores. Up until 22 September 2009, the AFM had intercepted or rescued 1314 irregular migrants. The Maltese Government has lobbied the EU for additional support and resources, particularly needed around the summer months, which constitute the peak period for arrivals.

The European Union has answered this call through Frontex, the European Agency for the Management of Operational Cooperation at the External Borders of the Member States of the European Union. Frontex is based in Warsaw and was established in 2005. In 2008, Frontex had its budget doubled to tackle the Mediterranean (Lutterbeck, 2009, p. 129). During Operation Nautilus in the Mediterranean off Malta, 2942 irregular migrants were intercepted in 69 days of operation (Communities, 2008). Little is known of Frontex's handling of irregular migrants or what happens to them following their apprehension. Despite this, the presence of Frontex has been considered a humanitarian advance over the previous efforts of Maltese fishermen and armed forces. The Head of the Fishing Association in Malta said that fishermen would "put the engine in full thrust" upon seeing a boatload of migrants so as not to lose a day's work (Lutterbeck, 2009, p. 132). International attention was focused on Malta when, in May 2007, 27 Africans were found clinging to tuna nets while Italy, Malta and Libya fought to avoid responsibility. The men were finally picked up by an Italian vessel and brought to safety (Ostergaard, 2008).

Sovereignty has a new place in the Maltese national consciousness as the perceived threat posed by irregular migration is sensationalised in the media. Asylum seekers are portrayed as diseased and criminal, a perception implicitly supported by the government's mandatory detention policy.

The policies of the government have led the European Commission against Racism and Intolerance (ECRI, 2008, p. 27) to express the concern that:

> The policies put in place by the Maltese authorities to respond to the challenges of irregular immigration into the country are seriously reinforcing perceptions of immigrants as criminals and increasing the levels of racism and xenophobia among the general population.

The preamble to its key policy brief of departments responsible for asylum seekers uses words and phrases that indicate the heightened vulnerability of Malta. It uses terms such as, "the fight against irregular migration", and makes clear that "the cooperation and collaboration of all EU Member States are necessary so as to ensure equitable *burden* sharing". It recognises that "Malta is in a truly vulnerable position" (MJHA & MFSS, 2005). Statistics as at 2006 indicated that the average annual arrival numbers were equivalent to 45% of the annual birthrate (LIBE, 2006, p. 3), a statistic often cited by government officials. As a result of this perception of Malta's vulnerability to the threat of immigration, the integration of asylum seekers and those who have received successful determinations was not on the government's agenda until very recently. Integration has also been hampered by the fact that most arrivals in Malta never intended on reaching Malta and instead were hoping to reach Italy.

Up until 2000, Malta was without a domestic refugee-processing framework. Despite signing the Refugee Convention in 1971, the government opted to outsource its refugee determination procedures to UNHCR (MJHA & MFSS, 2005; Amore, 2007). In passing the *Refugee Act 2000,* the Maltese Government created the Office of the Refugee Commissioner and the Refugee Appeals Board. This new national system operated autonomously in processing and making determinations on applications for refugee status from 2002 onwards (MJHA, 2009). Malta has been criticised for its treatment of irregular migrants by various human rights organisations and EU institutions. More recently, its questionable conduct of search-and-rescue operations has drawn condemnation (Ostergaard, 2008). The rising incidence of racism and xenophobia is also seen as a reflection of government inaction.

The number of people arriving by boat in Malta has increased dramatically since the early 2000s: the 2008 total was almost 50 times the 2001 number of arrivals at the start of the decade (NSO, 2009). Statistics in the Maltese context are difficult to obtain as record keeping is limited and the system is still in a nascent stage. We sought to obtain a gender breakdown of these statistics from the Office of the Commissioner for Refugees but no statistics were recorded. In addition, NGOs have expressed concern at the number of irregular migrants turned away at the airport, yet statistics on this number are also unavailable (LIBE, 2006; NSO, 2009). In order to put the increased influx of arrivals into context, in 2007 there were 51,000 arrivals along Europe's southern borders, including the coastlines of Spain, Greece, Italy and Malta (Ostergaard, 2008). The Maltese share is but a tiny slice of the overall number, but authorities argue that in proportion to the country's population, the numbers are significant. The southern borders of the European Union constitute the primary countries of entry to the EU. UNHCR states that, in the first half of 2009, arrivals in Europe's southern region occupied three quarters of all arrivals into Europe (UNHCR, 2010).

The surge of arrivals in Malta corresponds with similar increases in Sicily and Lampedusa (Lutterbeck, 2009, p. 122) and then the decline in arrivals since the outsourcing agreements with Libya have come into full force in mid 2010. Although research has yet to shed definitive light on the complexity of migration routes, Lutterbeck speculates that the strengthening of border protection policies in other key areas along Europe's southern border, such as Spain and Italy, has affected this massive increase in Malta. Lutterbeck contends that migration routes have shifted from the former route through Albania to Italy via the Adriatic Sea, as a result of Italian policing deterrents along the Adriatic coast (Lutterbeck, 2009, p. 122). The success of Spanish policing efforts off the Canary Islands is also said to have contributed to the number of West Africans arriving in Malta (Lutterbeck, 2009, p. 123). Since 2008 larger boats have been used in preference to the smaller boats used in the past. These larger boats carry over 250 people, compared to the previously used fishing vessels or tailor-made rubber dinghies which could carry no more than 30 persons. The perception was that the larger boats move more quickly and carry more persons, making it a more lucrative operation for smugglers. In mid-2009, in the run-up to the Italian elections, boats ceased arriving in Malta most likely as a result of Italian Government pressure on Libya to prevent boats from leaving the Libyan coast.

A focus on advising arrivals of their rights for asylum has also led to significant increases in the percentage of people who have applied for asylum. Prior to 2005, the Jesuit Refugee Service of Malta found that people arriving by boat were given insufficient information regarding their right to apply for asylum (JRS, 2006). This is particularly crucial given that arrivals are only allowed a two-month window in which to apply for asylum, although this can be extended in certain circumstances (JRS, 2006, p. 7). Communication between immigration authorities and new arrivals has also improved recently. The Office of the Refugee Commissioner has adopted a practice of providing information on how to apply for asylum and distributing this in several languages (ECRI, 2008, p. 17).

In 2008, the bulk of applicants were coming from the Horn of Africa countries: Somalia, Eritrea and Ethiopia. A considerable number have also been arriving from West Africa: the Ivory Coast, Ghana, Mali and Nigeria. The clear majority of asylum applicants come from Somalia (see Table 2.1).

In previous years a greater number of asylum seekers came from Iraq and other parts of the Middle East (UNHCR, 2005). Moreover, Somali women comprise a higher proportion of Somali arrivals than do women of any other country of origin.

Although arriving unauthorised in Malta is no longer a criminal offence, Malta has a system of compulsory detention for all unauthorised arrivals. Policy documents suggest that the rationale behind mandatory detention is linked to the national interest, "and more specifically, for reasons concerning employment, accommodation and maintenance of public order" (MJHA & MFSS, 2005, p. 6). Malta has had a policy of compulsory detention since 1970.

Up until 2005, people could be detained indefinitely. Indeed, some people had been in detention for more than five years before the policy was amended to set a time limit (LIBE, 2006, p. 2). People are now meant to be detained for a maximum of either 12 (if they have applied for asylum and are waiting on a determination) or 18 months (for those who have had their claim rejected or did not apply for asylum in the first instance); yet there are reports of people being kept beyond the 18-month

Table 2.1 Applications for asylum by citizenship in 2008 (NSO, 2009)

Citizenship	Male	Female	Total
Burkina Faso	33	0	33
Ivory Coast	262	0	262
Eritrea	153	22	175
Ethiopia	78	19	97
Gambia	44	0	44
Ghana	106	1	107
Guinea	39	0	39
Guinea-Bissau	8	0	8
Liberia	24	1	25
Mali	209	0	209
Niger	93	1	94
Nigeria	172	52	224
Senegal	15	0	15
Sierra Leone	19	4	23
Somalia	875	207	1082
Sudan	30	0	30
Togo	70	1	71
Other Africa	30	4	34
Other countries	29	7	36

maximum (LISE, 2006, p. 2; ECRI, 2008). In Southern European states Spain and Italy, people are detained for 40 days and 60 days, respectively (Ostergaard, 2008, p. 14). UNHCR believes Malta's policy is the strictest in Europe by a considerable margin (UNHCR, 2009). The maximum length of detention permitted is a policy decision and is not covered by legislation—a matter that has alarmed refugee advocates (ICJ, 2008). The mandatory detention policy for "prohibited immigrants" also breaches Article 5 of the European Charter on Human Rights which states that detention is only allowable in two circumstances: to prevent unauthorised entry into the county or when action is being taken with a view to deportation or extradition. Malta has refused to sign other European instruments related to migrants (ECRI, 2008, p. 7).

4.1 Detention Centres

At present there are six detention centres and 14 Open Centres on Malta. Three detention centres are run by the armed forces and three by the police (LISE, 2006). An army colonel has oversight of all closed centres. The Detention Service was established in 2005 to bring the military and police management of detention centres under joint command. The Maltese Government has committed to replacing military and police roles with civilians, but this is yet to happen. The government claims that all personnel have had human rights training; however, there are reports of a heavy emphasis on security and control in place of human rights and dignity (ECRI, 2008; Ostergaard, 2008).

Conditions in detention in Malta have been deplorable for women. Single women have been forced to share living quarters with single men, and both government and non-government agencies attest to significant rates of pregnancy in detention. Until relatively recently no contraception was distributed in detention centres. There has been a suggestion that women have resorted to pregnancy as a way to gain release from the closed centres and be relocated to open centres, as single women are not classified as vulnerable. People categorised as "vulnerable persons" may be released from detention centres into Open Centres. "Vulnerable persons" refers to "elderly persons, persons with a disability, lactating mothers and pregnant women" (ECRI, 2008, p. 13). A recent report by the European Commission against Racism and Intolerance found that waiting periods for assessments could extend into months (2008, p. 15).

The perpetration of sexual violence and forced pregnancies in detention centres has been compounded by the extensive system of gendered social control in Malta. Malta is intensely Catholic (Scicluna & Knepper, 2008). The marriage laws of Malta contain no provision for divorce. Abortion is illegal and there is little access to sexual health education (HRC, 2009, p. 9). In its report of 2009, the UN Human Rights Council urged Malta to amend its Civil Code, which presently distinguishes between "legitimate" and "illegitimate" children (HRC, 2009, p. 5). "Legitimate" children have more rights than those born outside of wedlock (HRC, 2009, p. 5). Malta has one of the lowest employment rates for women: 34.9% for women, compared to 74.5% for men (Eurostat, 2008, p. 256). In 2008, the proportion of female members of parliament was 9.2% (UNSD, 2008). A significant emphasis on the family has meant that women are largely confined to, and defined by, that context. To illustrate the point, in Malta's Criminal Code rape falls under the title "Of Crimes against the Peace and Honour of Families and Morals" (HRC, 2009, p. 6).

The state of detention centres in Malta has been criticised by numerous groups including the European Committee for the Prevention of Torture, the Council of Europe Commissioner for Human Rights, the European Parliaments Committee on Civil Liberties and Human Rights, Amnesty International, Medicine de Monde, and *Médicins Sans Frontières* (MSF). MSF opted to pull out of Malta in protest at conditions in 2008. Lyster Barracks, one of the detention centres visited by the Rapporteur from the Committee on Civil Liberties, Justice and Home Affairs (LIBE, 2006, p. 8), was described as follows:

> The centre is run by military personnel and accommodates up to 230 people. A large number of tents have also been erected to house migrants outside. In each tent there are about 20 beds and only one small heater. Some beds are used as cupboards because there is very little space.
> In the actual centre itself the living conditions are appalling. Men and women live together in extremely tight spaces. In one room there are two married couples living together, each couple sleeping in a single bed, as well as two single girls. The delegation met women who were four months pregnant and an old woman. At the entrance to the centre there is a prison for migrants guilty of some misdemeanour. One of them, a deaf mute, is accused of hitting his wife. There are only two functioning toilets for more than 100 people. The migrants have organised shifts for cleaning. The hygiene conditions and the overcrowding are intolerable. The women are not given any sanitary towels. Here, too, people are given

out-of-date drugs and poor quality food, and they are not allowed to go out. There is not even an outside area at this centre.

The same Rapporteur found that there were no activities available for detainees. The need for qualified staff is of greater importance in this context because the population has health or psychological problems as a result of having experienced trauma. Conditions in the detention centres are said to be difficult for both the detainees and the guards (LIBE, 2006, p. 5). Although some observers have remarked that services in these detention centres have improved with the advent of private management, Medicine de Monde and MSF have been critical of the conditions and the healthcare available (Ostergaard, 2008). Detainees must clean the centres themselves (LIBE, 2006). The UN Working Group on Arbitrary Detention visited two of the detention centres: Safi and Lyster. It found conditions to be "appalling to the extent that the health, including mental health, of the detainees is affected". They went on to say:

> The sub-standard closed centres of Safi and Lyster Barracks are overcrowded. At Lyster Barracks, families are not separated from men, women, including pregnant and nursing mothers, and children, including unaccompanied minors. Although the Government applies a fast track procedure for the release of vulnerable groups in administrative detention, the procedures may take several months and be in vain for those who are considered a health risk. Many dwell in tents and the Working Group notes with serious concern that 59 inmates do not even find a place to sleep in these tents at present. (WAGD, 2009, p. 4)

As recently as 2007 a UNHCR report found that:

> Malta's detention policy is also at times applied to vulnerable persons, namely children, pregnant and lactating women, elderly persons, persons with disabilities and victims of torture and trauma. The procedure for fast-tracked release of these vulnerable persons from detention often suffers from administrative hindrances, resulting in unnecessarily long detention and related negative consequences for the vulnerable persons. Whilst in detention, minors, including children, do not generally receive any kind of education and are only permitted minimal time for leisure activities in the open air. Female, male and minor asylum-seekers are not segregated, but accommodated in the same premises and with joint use of showers and toilets.
>
> The medical service provided in detention is not sufficient to meet all the needs, often urgent, of the detained asylum-seekers. Health risks are also present due to the severe hygiene conditions and lack of ventilation. The Detention Service also makes extensive use of inappropriate cells for the confinement of asylum-seekers as a means of punishment, and use of violence and offensive language, including threats, is common in the centres. (UNHRC, 2007, p. 5)

4.2   Open Centres

Open Centres are run either by state or non-state organisations for several categories of people: people released from detention after 12 months who have not yet had their asylum claim decided; those who have been released after 18 months of detention; and those who have had their asylum claims approved. If people's asylum claims are not settled after 12 months they are granted certain working rights.

In order to participate in the labour market people are transferred from detention to Open Centres. People are only allowed to stay in an Open Centre for up to one year, after which time their financial assistance is cut off (Masurelle & Poykko, 2007). Men are still housed in tent-style accommodation in Hal-Far Open Centre, and there is a converted hanger that also houses asylum seekers. Those in Open Centres are given an allowance of € 2.30 for every child and 4.60 for each adult (Masurelle & Poykko, 2007). If they leave the Open Centre and access the private market they lose both this allowance and their ability to return to an Open Centre. There are a great number of people living in Open Centres who have been denied any sort of humanitarian protection. In 2006, this number was put at 800 (UBE, 2006, p. 2).

There are three types of protection available to those who arrive in Malta and seek asylum. Firstly, applications are assessed on the basis of refugee status. Failing that, asylum seekers may be entitled to "subsidiary protection", otherwise known as humanitarian protection. According to the government's website, subsidiary protection "applies to failed asylum seekers, who if returned to their country of origin would face a real risk of suffering serious harm" (MJHA, 2009, p. 3). The subsidiary protection scheme was introduced in 2008 following an EU Council Directive.[2] The third category of protection is temporary humanitarian protection, which is available to those who do not qualify for refugee status or subsidiary protection, but are deemed worthy of temporary protection. This is re-evaluated on a yearly basis. The Refugee Commissioner said that those given this protection are generally minors or have medical problems.

4.3   Subsidiary Protection

According to the Office for the Commissioner of Refugees, on average 70% of extra legal arrivals apply for refugee status and 47% receive some kind of humanitarian protection, but a mere 3% receive refugee status (Ostergaard, 2008, p. 29). In 2008, for example, 19 people received refugee status whereas 1394 received subsidiary protection (MJHA, 2009, p. 6). This amounts to 0.07% of applicants receiving refugee status, and 50% receiving subsidiary protection.

Those with subsidiary protection are given one-year residence permits that are renewable. They are able to receive travel documents, to work, to receive welfare benefits, healthcare and access to education and integration programs. Dependants, if they are in Malta at the time the protection is granted, have the same rights and benefits as the primary holders. This assistance is provided to people until they re-settle in a third country or are able to return to their countries of origin. Subsidiary protection has generated a great deal of criticism among refugee experts who query whether it is assigning a label to avoid recognising the rights of refugees (Hathaway, 2003). Subsidiary protection provides a formula for humanitarian protection that is temporary.

---

[2] EU Council Directive 2004/83 EC.

4.4 Dublin II Treaty

Essentially, the first Dublin Treaty outlined the common asylum application pro-cedure. It sets out the criteria for determining the member state for processing the asylum applications of third-country nationals. It also established "Eurodac", a fin-gerprint system that enables asylum seekers to be identified. Malta is one of the few European nations that fingerprints asylum seekers. Dublin II stipulated that the responsibility lies with the country in which the applicants first make their ap-plication for asylum. Although Malta complies with Dublin II, it has not received favourable treatment. The Maltese Government has criticised the Treaty, arguing that it was forced to share too much of the burden and that the Treaty favours other countries that do not receive as many asylum seekers. As a result, those who arrive on Malta's shores do not have the right to apply for asylum in another EU country. The Maltese authorities have sought an exemption from the Dublin II regulation based on the argument that they are handling a disproportionate share of Europe's asylum applications (LIBE, 2006).

5 Conclusion

Women's experiences of crossing borders, including their experience of violence for both opportunistic and political or organised ends, have dramatically shaped the ways in which they cross borders to flee conflict. By studying women's experiences from Mogadishu to Malta, we can see that such violence manifests in different ways, but is all part of a changing landscape of violence that is effective in prevent-ing women from crossing from the Global South to the Global North, and which in essence punishes them for arriving unauthorised in the Global North. Gender-based violence, and rape in particular, has been used for political, cultural and social ends for it has consequences not only for individual women, but also for families and clans, in a range of conflicts involving local, national and regional actors.

   If we begin with women's stories of flight and border crossing it becomes ap-parent that there is rarely a singular border crossing in the journey to their destina-tion. Rather, there are many crossings of both internal and external borders, which often do not map onto the sovereign territorial borders on which developed nations continue to focus their enforcement efforts. The violence women experience before, during and after extra legal border crossing occurs along a continuum of harm, most of which goes unnoticed at the formal territorial border crossing. Moreover, the continuums of the crossings women make are only possible through their risking serious violence in flight, transit and reception. Fleeing persecution, serious harm, threat of violence or insufferable poverty often requires submitting or at least risk-ing those same or greater harms in order to escape. This chapter has evidenced that women's extra legal border crossings are numerous and ongoing, and throughout the continuum those who police their crossings include both opportunists and organised interests who rely in concert and individually on practices of sexual violence. The control of women who cross borders in Africa is overwhelmingly performed by non-government agents, using an array of gender-based acts of violence to achieve ends that are either organisational or individual. Finally, European-based forms of border control, in this case those of Malta, regularly use institutional violence as a frontline strategy in deterring and punishing forced migrants.

6 Summary

This chapter focuses on women's experiences of border enforcement when fleeing conflict from Somalia, through Libya and Kenya and reception in Malta. It is concerned with the ways both state and non-state violence act as the most effective forms of control over women. Such violence includes gender-based violence by militia, government agents and institutions. Somalia has been regarded as a failure among failed states, yet at the same time depictions of lawlessness do not adequately account for experiences of control over women's mobility. Malta has been on the frontline of European attempts to reject extra legal migration and has been subject to extensive criticism for warehousing of refugees in appalling conditions.

Chapter 3
Border Policing in the Borderlands: Policing Politically Active Women on the Thai–Burma Border

Extra legal border crossing is often considered a particular moment of physical transgression in a linear journey across clearly marked territorial sovereign borders. Based on this assumption, it is reasonable to expect that the policing of border crossing can be focused on a temporally and spatially contained moment. What 15 years of research in the field has taught me is that most border crossings last a lifetime, as does their policing. For many, border crossing is not just a moment, or an hour, or half a day that it takes to cross the point which on internationally recognised maps indicates the end of one state's territory and the beginning of another. Rather, border crossing involves the process of evading authorities in approaching a specific cartographically marked line (or an approximation of where such a line is located), followed by a period of time in limbo—a limbo marked by extra legal status, or precarious migration status. Refugees often spend years living in camps, buffer zones or other areas geographically proximate to the cartographic border but somehow not yet in the destination country, and not entirely removed from their country of origin.

The Thai–Burma border is one such place—where a borderland is recognisable and where border crossings last lifetimes. Interviews with politically active women living and working in the borderland evidence the need to expand narrow conceptions of border policing to consider the complex relationships and policing practices that exert control and facilitate movement in these peculiar spaces. This chapter focuses on a particular group of women: those who have overtly engaged in political processes for democracy in Burma, including women active in the Bamar, Karen, Kachin and Shan communities. In this regard, this is no ordinary group of women, as they have crossed a border and live in compromised circumstances, and include women who have been active in carving out a space for women's political voices to be heard and are daily involved in improving their communities.

S. Pickering, *Women, Borders, and Violence,*
DOI 10.1007/978-1-4419-0271-9_3, © Springer Science+Business Media, LLC 2011

1   The Transversal Borderland

The performance of modern statecraft is often understood as constituted by a series of state practices (primarily through the use of state power, institutions and representatives) that enact and enforce state boundaries central to the performance of state sovereignty (Devetak, 1995, 2001; Doty, 1996). Whereas sovereignty has traditionally been conceived as demarcating a natural inside from a natural outside, with spatially and temporally fixed definitions, more recently it has come to be understood as underpinned by historically and politically normalised interpretations of the state that are neither natural nor neutral (Reus-Smit, 2001). Rather than viewing sovereignty as having a fixed essence, it is increasingly considered a performance of the state (or practice of statecraft) (Soguk, 1999; Doty, 1996; Weber, 1995). As such, violent boundary inscription practices undertaken by the state against the refugee can be understood as a form of statecraft. The pursuit of such practices seeks to create a political space in a "boundary producing political performance" which in turn brings into being the sovereign state (Devetak, 1995). The concept of statecraft moves a criminological understanding of border policing from a position of the border as fixed to the border as spatially produced and circulated, as part of a process in which policing plays a critical role. The state is not only constituted by violence (Tilly, 1985), but also maintained through violent boundary-inscription practices. National borders are no longer seen as lines on a map but as marking spaces of both legitimate and illegitimate behaviour, which require simultaneous performances of control and crisis that collapse boundaries, frontiers and borders into borderlands. I have been concerned with how such boundary-policing political performance as a form of statecraft is experienced and negotiated by certain groups (arguably privileged groups of the political class).

Nevins has argued that political geography may differentiate boundaries, frontiers and borders in the following way:

> A boundary [is a] strict line of separation between two (at least theoretically) distinct territories, a frontier is a forward zone of contact with the uncontrolled or sparsely settled, and a border is an area of interaction and gradual division between two separate political entities. (Nevins, 2002, p. 8)

According to such a definition the Thai–Burma border is somewhere between a frontier and a border. However, there is a body of literature that suggests that prior to reaching any such understanding the condition of transversality must be recognised, which does not occupy a space between boundaries, frontiers and borders (sovereign or otherwise) but rather exists "Prior to the conventional sovereign boundaries that enable political inclusions, exclusions and cultural separations across peoples and places" (Soguk & Whitehall, 1999, p. 675). The transversal, Soguk and Whitehall argue, is defined both for and by migrants and movements. Central to the concept of transversality is the idea that sovereign boundaries/frontiers/borders are themselves temporary, and in fact constitute an example of transversality itself. Underpinning transversality are a range of processes, including border crossing and de-territorialisation (Glissant, 1989). Critiquing the dominant spatially centric approach of international relations scholarship, Soguk and Whitehall argue that the concept of transversality does not start with the state as the central agent in life but with the transversal. Transversality takes the voices of migrants as the starting point in disrupting state-centric narratives of sovereignty and borders, as well as the potential of individuals to be alternative legal/political/social subjects in realms where previously they were territorially bounded and silenced. Therefore, applying the concept of transversality would not begin with the accounts of state agents such as border police charged with the policing of transversal spaces.[1]

In the borderlands there often exists a web of informal practices that draw on traditional practices of law, law enforcement and security that run counter to the application (or absence of application) of international law—particularly in relation to refugee protection. This chapter explores the ways in which women negotiate everyday living in borderland communities through their negotiations with policing bodies.

2 Burma

In October 2007 the United Nations Human Rights Council issued a statement deploring the repression in Burma. The Burmese junta violently responded to protests led by Buddhist monks against escalating commodity prices. The monks demanded dialogue and the release of political prisoners, (ICG, 2008) and the United States and the EU along with other nations issued or renewed sanctions against the Burmese regime. Leading international non-government organisations, such as the International Committee of the Red Cross, have not been permitted to work in Burma since 2006. In 2007, the Burmese regime placed further restrictions on international agencies and the United Nations. NGO activity within Burma is necessarily covert; Human Rights Watch recently reported that in the ethnic areas of the borderlands human rights violations remain widespread, and include sexual violence against women and girls, forced labour and summary executions (HRW, 2008). Between 2006 and 2008, 40,000 civilians were displaced in Karen State. The borderlands have become increasingly militarised, with the Burmese military erecting 43 new bases in Karen border areas.

Burma has been ranked 190 of 191 countries in the Social Watch analysis of healthcare delivery,[2] and its lack of social and infrastructure spending is parlous compared with its expenditure on the military (estimated at 30–50% of state spending). The most recent reports available from within Burma indicate that living conditions continue to deteriorate despite the impending elections and slight increases in access to the international community following Cyclone Nargis. It is the situation within Burma that has driven so many to seek a future outside Burma. As is now widely recognised:

---

[1] Sections of this page are taken from Pickering, 2004.

[2] www.socwatch.org.uy/en/fichasPais/ampliado_137.html.

...migration from Burma, both within the country and across the border, has become a cultural phenomenon because it is not exclusive to the most marginalized and oppressed but has become a cultural norm in nearly all walks of life in Burma and is something in which people from all different regions of Burma partake. In addition, migration itself has been transformed from an economically driven process to one of survival from crushing poverty and human rights abuses. (BWU, 2007, p. 9)

The United Nations and international non-government organisations have registered significant ongoing concern over human rights abuses occurring at Burma's borders, where thousands of ethnic minorities have fled seeking an end to persecution and repression.

Through research with 140 women who have fled Burma for China and Thailand, the Burmese Women's Union (BWU) has documented how refugees and migrants have become indistinguishable as all groups leave Burma to escape the oppressive State Peace and Development Council (SPDC) regime. However, the reality of the border crossing does depend on where individuals fall within what has been termed the "hierarchical culture of migration" from Burma, which is shaped by the economic status, social status, relationship with the SPDC, ethnicity and sex of the migrant (BWU, 2007). The final destination of a migrant or refugee from Burma, and their success in terms of social mobility, is largely determined by their position in the three-tier system of migration and their circumstances in Burma prior to leaving. The BWU has recently reported that those in the worst situations often move at the bottom of the hierarchy while the most affluent and/or influential move at the top. This hierarchy determines whether someone fleeing Burma is able to migrate to a developed nation or is left in limbo in a neighbouring developing country.

The three-tier system of migration is categorized according to the level of safety and mobility attached to working conditions and employment opportunities available to the migrant. Thus, each ascending level represents or signifies better prospects for the migrant than the previous level. Migrants in the top/first tier tend to be a limited number and a small group of individuals compared to the bottom tier, as they are a minority group of individuals within poverty-stricken Burma, who have a significant amount of affluence and education. Therefore, they are able to find the means of migrating to their host countries that are developed countries of the Global North. Furthermore, this group of migrants is able to use their affluence to leave Burma through conventional channels, holding legal passports and valid visas. It is worth noting that while desperate migrants who migrate for survival must work in their host countries, affluent migrants of the first tier have migrated to further their education and/or to seek permanent settlement. Migrants who constitute the second tier make up a larger group than the first tier due to a combination of factors: closer proximity, bi-lateral agreements, laxer entry restrictions in countries such as Japan and Singapore. Characteristics of migrants in this group are quite similar to those of the first tier in terms of affluence and education. The only difference between the two tiers is often an increase in migrating volume, poorer working conditions and migrant labor rights. (BWU, 2007)

Of greatest importance here in understanding this pyramid of migration is that all groups are dominated by male migrants. As research by the BWU has demonstrated, women are unable to travel freely because of official limitations on women's national and international travel. The SPDC does not permit women (16–25 years old) to travel alone—they must travel in the company of a legal guardian. These regulations were introduced and defended as measures to combat trafficking into the sex industry. They sit alongside restrictions on women travelling for educational purposes without government approval. Identity cards are required for travel in and out of Burma, but these are often prohibitively expensive for women to access. As the BWU has concluded: "These travel restrictions combined with poor economic conditions leave women with no choice but to become irregular migrant workers migrating at the bottom of the three-tier system", often fleeing Burma because migration has become the "culturally predominant" means of survival (BWU, 2007, p. 11). Women flee Burma because of extreme poverty, lack of a future inside Burma under the military regime and/or familial obligation:

> ...there is usually no clear-cut distinction between the aforementioned reasons and in fact, these three factors interlink and compel women and girls to leave their country and maintain Burma's culture of migration. (BWU, 2007, p. 20)

Burma ranks 132 out of 177 on the UNDP's Human Development Index.[3] It is home to a civil war that has raged for the last four decades. The Burmese Constitution was ratified by the people in a controversial 2008 vote that took place immediately following Cyclone Nargis, while relief work was still in its early stages. Although 92% of the 98% of voters who turned out reportedly said "yes" to the new Constitution, some independent election observers have raised doubts over the legitimacy of the process (ICG, 2009). The Constitution provides the military with 25% of the seats in Parliament—a move that has entrenched their role in government. Burma has been under military rule since 1962.

Following the 2010 elections Aung San Suu Kyi, leader of the Opposition National League for Democracy was released from house arrest which she had experienced for 14 of the last 20 years. The 2010 elections were widely regarded as a sham, with the military retaining of 75% of the seats in parliament and many groups being disenfranchised.

In late September 2007, Buddhist monks led protests through the streets of Yangon. This constituted the most public display of dissent since the 1988 protests were violently repressed by the then government. The 2007 crackdown was precipitated by rising commodity prices dramatically increased the cost of living. In particular, the cost of fuel surged, suspending bus routes and local transport systems. Initially protests continued unhindered and many people joined the monks in protest. After monks were beaten by non-state actors in Pakkoku, south-west of Mandalay, the All Burma Monks Alliance was formed, who demanded a decrease in commodity prices, the release of political prisoners and the commencement of a dialogue with the opposition. A curfew was later imposed by the regime, and troops sealed off the streets before monasteries were raided and monks taken to detention centres. The authorities used tear gas, batons, rubber bullets and live ammunition on the crowds. Nine people were killed, one of whom was a Japanese photographer. People were taken to interrogation centres (ICG, 2008, p. 3). Some of those sentenced as a result of the crackdown received 65-year sentences (ICG, 2009, p. 1).

---

[3] UNDP (2007) Human Development Index Report at http://hdrstats.undp.org/countries/country_fact_sheets/cty_fs_MMR.html (Accessed 5 December 2008).

Cyclone Nargis, a Category 4 cyclone, is believed to be the worst recorded natural disaster in Myanmar's history. On 2 May 2008, it struck the Irrawaddy delta region, 250 km south-west of Yangon, and worked its way inland, reaching Yangon late that night (ICG, 2008). Winds of up to 200 km/h and tidal surges up to 4 m high caused widespread devastation (ICG, 2008). The exact numbers of people affected or killed are difficult to obtain but estimates suggest that 84,537 people were killed, with another 53,836 missing, presumed dead (TCG, 2008).

The cyclone had many impacts on the country. A Tripartite Core Group was established to govern the relief effort, involving the UA, the Association of Southeast Asian Nations (ASEAN) and the Government of Myanmar. The first of its kind, this arrangement saw unprecedented cooperation by the Government of Myanmar. The situation created increased space in which civil society could organise, and more donors contributed to the country (CPCS, 2008).

Ceasefire agreements were developed in several of the border regions. They are currently negotiating to transform the ceasefire groups into a Border Guard Force, which will involve a system whereby the armed groups come under the central command of the military (Kramer, 2009). This has led to renewed outbreaks of fighting in some areas (BBC, 2009). The United States now acknowledges that sanctions have failed to bring about change and is instead pursuing increased engagement with Myanmar in a bid to influence democratic reform. It has yet to dispense with sanctions (Reuters, 2009).

Some reports suggest that economic sanctions have shut down large parts of the garment industry, resulting in an increase in the number of women entering the sex industry. While not meaning to confuse the two issues, it is noteworthy that since Cyclone Nargis there has been an increase in the number of organisations accessing funds to address sex trafficking within and from Burma.

3   The Thai–Burma Border

The Thai–Burma border has been the site of hundreds of thousands of unauthorised crossings over the past 30 years resulting from the repression of the military junta in Burma. As a consequence, a series of camps have been set up inside Thailand where refugees from Burma are able to live, without the protection of the UN Refugee Convention to which Thailand is not a signatory. In addition, there is an effective zone of approximately 20 km inland from the Burmese border into Thailand in which so-called illegal immigrants, if apprehended, are not automatically sent back over the river or the mountains into Burma.

There are 14 refugee camps along the Thai–Burma border. While Thailand is not a signatory to the 1951 UN Refugee Convention it is bound by international customary law in relation to *refoulement*. The Thai Government recognises refugees only if they flee directly from armed conflict, are officially granted (persons of concern) status by UNHCR, or are housed within refugee camps along the border.

Far larger numbers of people live outside the camps. In addition, it is estimated that in excess of two million people from Burma are migrant workers in neighbouring countries. Recently, Thailand has deported tens of thousands Laotian Hmong refugees, despite international outcry over the conditions to which they are returning (Kittiwongsakul, 2009).

Thailand has previously permitted international bodies such as UNHCR and IOM to conduct refugee determinations in Thai camps. The Provincial Admissions Board (the Thai agency that ascertains asylum claims) has reportedly been abandoned. The Thai authorities work to prevent thousands of refugees from entering Thailand. Human Rights Watch has reported that refugees from Shan State in Burma are being routinely denied entry into Thailand, alongside increasing reports of refugees being forced back over the border in 2007 and 2008. Human Rights Watch has also reported that Rohingya Muslims arriving from Burma into Southern Thailand are being routinely arrested by Thai security forces and *refouled* to Burma. In addition to the active border enforcement efforts of Thai authorities, restrictions on migrant workers from Burma have dramatically increased, with the authorities now utilising curfews and restrictions on telecommunications against migrant workers who are routinely subject to arbitrary arrest, harassment and detention. Women are part of the ongoing small trading that takes place across the border, whereby people continually cross back and forth to collect and trade materials, food and other goods. Recent reports evidence that corrupt practices mean they must pay Burmese officials for this passage. There are conflicting reports that women are finding it easier to negotiate these crossing points with officials and others suggest that women are more vulnerable.

3.1 Experiences with Police in Burma

Women's experiences of policing in the borderland are shaped by their experiences of violence within Burma, including the events precipitating their border crossing. For many women, violence in Burma is often at the hands of state-sponsored agencies, often the military but also the police and police-like bodies, including ceasefire groups, along the border. For most politically active women, their initial contact with police in Burma follows their participation in student politics and/or the broader democracy movement. The women interviewed for this research had all taken part in protests on 8 August 1988 and many attested to this bringing them into direct contact, and indeed confrontation, with police. For some women this had resulted in arrest and detention. While still in Burma many women had fought against strict family control over their political activism. Some women also had to negotiate traditional family expectations regarding the duty to honour the family, especially the wishes of the father, as well as social expectations that educated people should gain respectable employment in the public service. However, other women we interviewed described how there is a long history of discrimination against ethnic minorities in the public service. The authorities have utilised gender social mores during arrest and interrogation to maximise the pressure they can exert on women in the extraction of information about their political activities and the activities of others:

> After they sent me to jail they started to investigate me. Intelligence came and took me to the main jail. The whole day they asked many, many questions. They insulted our character. The first technique is to attack the character. For example, they accused me that I had slept two nights in the big hall already: "How can you stay with boys?" Mostly women are very angry when they are insulted like that. They accused me of staying very mixed with men: "I don't believe you didn't stay like husband and wife!", they said like that. I was so angry at first…. The second time he threatened to punch me in the head: "If you don't answer I will punch you!" But I still stayed quiet. So he beat me with a stick on the back of the head, I felt so much pain but I still said nothing. So they changed the man…. At that time I was very lucky they did not try to sexually harass me…. (Respondent 1)

Many women had to deal with police in the rural and regional provinces where the involvement of authorities in the drug trade and the exploitation of human and natural resources have been widely reported (UNODC, 2010b).

> I have many friends, mostly boys, sometimes they want to trade opium. The police want to tax in some areas and when they go to that area, they have to pay the tax. With the jade work—this is sure because my brother worked in the jade dealing, not mining—my brother wanted to trade somewhere, in particular areas he had to pay the police. If they do not pay money they will be arrested…in many areas it was usually controlled by the soldier, because our area was a "brown" area. I stayed in this area until I was 18. I never respected the police. The police request money from people, this I know. At that time, until 1988, I respect the soldier, the military. Because the military try to get freedom and independence from Britain. My experience is also that in my area is the Kachin Independence Army. Sometimes they came to the town and the soldiers fought hem. I thought the soldiers were very brave, until 1988. (Respondent 4)

The government crackdown on the democracy movement in 1988, along with more recent crackdowns on protestors such as those that occurred across Burma in 2007 and 2008, saw tens of thousands of protestors flee to the jungle along the border. Conditions at the border have been marked by serious outbreaks of fighting, increasingly on the border with China about which concerns over drug trafficking and other illicit activities are increasing (ICG, 2009).

3.2 Crossing the Border

Crossing into Thailand from Burma is overwhelmingly a clandestine activity that carries significant risk. This is a risk that women and men repeatedly face while trying to avoid Thai and Burmese authorities as well as ceasefire groups. Most women cross the border multiple times. Sometimes this is because they have been deported to Burma by Thai authorities and they seek to return to Thailand. Sometimes it is because they need to see family who remain in Burma, including children. Whatever the reason, it was common for women to describe multiple border crossings.

Sometimes women utilise legitimate documents to cross into Thailand. These are often rejected by the authorities so women must resort to offering money to border checkpoint officials:

> I was stopped at the Mai Sai border—they saw my card was from Kachin State and I told them my story. My brother is working in Thailand and our grandmother is dying, and she wants to see him before she dies so I came to call my brother. But they don't believe me—I think they want money. I asked then what I can do for them. (Respondent 4)

Resorting to the use of fraudulent documents to fly to Thailand is possible if you have access to the financial and other resources required. The average wage in Burma is US \$200 per capita (USDOS, 2009) and the prohibitive price for fraudulent documents means most women who cross extra legally into Burma do so without documentation, using low-cost forms of transport such as buses and bicycles to travel to the border regions and walking and/or taking boats across into Thailand.

> It was very difficult for a woman to get a passport. But if you can pay 300000 Kyat you can get one. I tried to get my passport—finally I got it. I wanted to find a job, I wanted to get a job in Thailand. I flew on a plane with a legal passport. (Respondent 1)

Politically active women are more often, but not always, able to draw on material resources and organisational networks to facilitate their border crossing. For most women migrants such opportunities are far more difficult and often no other option than to attempt border crossings in hostile terrain.

The dense jungle and wide rivers of the border region mean that refugees fleeing Burma make and remake paths through inhospitable terrain. Clandestine crossings are often long and exhausting, requiring refugees to avoid the Burmese military on one side and the Thai authorities on the other.

> We walked—we had to leave from the village secretly. But there were many people on the road—there were high mountains but there was a car road. We walked for three days. I am not sure how many people were coming. If we rested there were more groups coming up behind us, continuously. Sometimes we saw Thais, police or soldiers. On the Thai side there was logging that we passed. When we arrived at the Thai side there was not a refugee camp, we settled in a small Mon village. After that we got to a refugee camp near Three Pagoda Pass—a Mon camp. There was no camp when we first arrived. (Respondent 2)

Research by the BWU has found that it is costly for women to travel out of Burma, and they are frequently forced to bribe checkpoint officials. Women often need to travel as part of a group or pay "carriers"[4] to smuggle them across the border and assist them in finding work in Thailand or other host countries. The role of carriers is often complex, for although they provide a much-needed service for women who have no other options, the power they have over the conditions of travel as well as work opportunities following arrival mean carriers wield a great deal of power over women. The BWU research revealed that often the price for travelling out of Burma is not negotiated until after departure from Burma, and opportunities for work are often misrepresented by carriers (BWU, 2007).

---

[4] The term "carriers" refers to people who go back and forth across the border facilitating clandestine crossings.

4 Policing Women's Activism

Once women arrive in Thailand their political activism often brings them into ongoing and complex relationships with policing and immigration agencies. One woman
described her experience at an education conference in Chiang Mai raided by Thai
police and immigration officials. The authorities flew people to Mae Hong Son
rather than directly deporting them.

> The intelligence and police came into the conference. They separated us into three groups:
> those with passports and legal papers; those with travelling documents and papers; and
> those who did not have anything. I was in the last group—I had nothing. At that time we
> cannot talk a lot. One woman could speak Thai and told them not to shout—and don't
> touch. The police told us to write our details: name, organisation and place of residence. At
> that time it was lunchtime and some people told the police that we wanted to eat. At that
> time they had blocked the exits to the room with chairs and the women told them that it was
> not legal to block the room for those with legal papers.

> Some of the police's faces were strong, and some were a little not too strong. At that time
> I know they would send us five people, without papers, to Mae Hong Son. I knew that we
> would not be arrested because the other two women discussed with intelligence, and the
> police said that their duty was only to send us to Mae Hong Son—they had promised—also
> they had discussed with another intelligence group that they would not do that. They flew us
> back to Mae Hong Son and we had to pay for the intelligence man for his plane charges. At
> Mae Hong Son airport they handed us over to the Mae Hong Son immigration. But it was 5
> pm in the day and they could not do the case that day, and we had to stay in the police station
> cell for the night—the police office instead of the immigration, why I don't know. But also
> every time the immigration send to the police station because they don't have a cell at immi-
> gration. In the morning two women came and said that if we paid money they would come
> and buy food for them. These women I think did this for money. At that time if we cannot
> pay then they feed us. The other women in the cell were migrants from Burma. Two of them
> could not buy, so they fed them, but not enough curry just a little bit. The other women were
> Shan who were working on farms near Mae Hong Son and the police arrested them because
> they had no ID cards. At 3 pm the next day the police called the immigration to make our
> case. We were worried—why did they take so long to call? But they said their immigration
> car was away and they could not come until the car come back, and if the car did not come
> back then we would have to stay another night in jail. We waited for the car until after 4 pm
> and then someone came and picked us up to take us to camp 2 at Ny Soi. They dropped us at
> Ny Soi because we paid 200 Baht for all. Cheap! At that time there was a KNOW women with
> us also, so all the opposition groups had worked together to negotiate us out. (Respondent 4)

5 Building Relationships with Intelligence

Women negotiate different border policing bodies in different ways. Often divergent strategies are used to effectively balance the power of one agency against the
mandate of another in women's efforts to achieve their goals. Consequently, women
must negotiate various layers of complex relationships with Thai authorities in the
process of their work and everyday lives. Although women's stories reveal multiple
forms of state control, the policing of women's activism is most pointed in relation

to restrictions on travel. Knowing what to do when confronted by one of these policing agencies depends on constant negotiation, experience and confidence building
over time.

> At the beginning we are always afraid of the Thai police and intelligence. Especially the
> police because we are illegal immigrants and they can check for our ID at any time. So if
> we want to go anywhere, we have to think a lot. At the beginning, every day, we can hear
> everywhere—who is arrested and where. (Respondent 6)

People are handled differently by the authorities depending on: their documentation (legal status); their gender; the circumstances in which they are confronted (for
example, the raid of a meeting or conference, or being picked up en route to another
destination); the culture of the location; where they are found (for example, on the
bus or in the street, in a high-level meeting with other colleagues, or in a prison
cell); their attitude and confidence levels; and their ability to communicate (for
example, in Thai and/or English). Women need to be confident and fearless without
being perceived as confrontational.

> Confidence is very important for us as a defence mechanism. It helps protect us at many
> levels. First, if we are confident, then we don't attract the attention of the authorities, they
> always look for who is not confident, who is not sure of what to do. Second, if we are
> arrested, and we are confident, we can negotiate better. Third, confidence is some—but
> not full—protection to stop officials approaching in a violent or sexually abusive manner.
> Confidence is one of the really important things…how to travel confidently. (Respondent 6)

Thai intelligence agencies are interested in information exchange: they want reports
of activities in return for permission to travel. This is not to suggest that any clear-
cut or hard and fast method of operational practice exists, but rather indicate the extent to which the authorities are able to monitor and shape women's activism in the
borderland. When considering strategies for travel, women must remain cognisant
of the broad patterns of policing practices. Unsurprisingly, policing practices differ
across locations, and the changes in personnel and practices across these locations
demand vigilant monitoring by women. Shifts in government policy and its impact
on the local political environment seriously affect women's capacity to operate. Due
to operational differences, however, one border area may be affected by these policies, whereas in other areas the same policy may be implemented quite differently.

Through listening to the women's stories offered in this research it became clear
that the various branches of the police and intelligence charged with policing the
border are often unaware of each other's operations. Intelligence agencies often cir-
cumnavigate police and immigration powers, highlighting the competition among
different intelligence agencies, the police, the Prime Minister's office and the army.
The women's stories also highlighted the difference in institutional cultures between the bureaucratic centre and the periphery. For example, when Bangkok police
units come to the border towns local security arrangements become ineffective.

> If the police were ever coming to the office then the intelligence would inform us before-
> hand so we need to hide reports and anything important for us—like the computer. When I
> was in Bangkok working for an NGO the police came. The director of the NGO talked with
> them. For us, we needed to hide in other rooms quietly. But the police said that they knew
> that there were illegal people in the office and warned that they would return the next day

and catch us. But we moved that night. Actually they didn't come. We stayed at a neighbour's house. But what the police did was tell the neighbours that if they saw illegal people at the house they would get 200 baht (if they told the police). (Respondent 2)

When we are told by intelligence we close the office down—but one or two women stay—but they must have papers and the rest of us are sent back to the camp until we are called back. (Respondent 5)

In building relationships with the most powerful agency—Thai intelligence—women's groups have been presented with some challenges stemming from the historically subservient role of women. Politically active women often needed to negotiate the macho practices of the intelligence world that is dominated by men. Traditionally, relationships between intelligence agencies and pro-democracy groups have been conducted between individual leaders and intelligence representatives in informal settings, relying on the development of rapport between men.

For the women's groups it is a little more difficult to form a relationship with the intelligence because most of the intelligence, they like to drink whiskey together like that. But our women in our culture we should not drink. But women should drink with people they know. So most of the women don't do that. So the women have a little difficulty to build the relationship. But the men can do this more easily, they are very happy to take this opportunity or responsibility. They spend a lot of money on the relationship with intelligence. (Respondent 6)

Politically active women also need to overcome a perception that they are not a serious or central part of the democracy movement and therefore worthy of interest. In short, they have significant information to trade and could benefit from the (albeit partial) protections Thai intelligence offer their lives and work in the borderlands:

I felt they [intelligence] are not interested a lot with the women's groups—"OK, you want to travel document?" OK they can give easily like that. But they think that women's groups are only for women's issues and not political issues. We know what kinds of information they want—we can give them. Buy they don't think we know it. It's a problem. They are always happy to meet a men's organisation because they think they will get some important information. The intelligence really cooperate with them. Sometimes they don't help us in the same way. For example, if we want to send three people to a conference maybe they will give papers for only one. (Respondent 6)

Police and intelligence used to come to the office and sometimes they took photos. Police used to come. Our organisation is with the men's office so they only talked with the men. But the police know there are also women. When the police came we had to hide. When I was in Chiang Mai there was a raid and everyone in the office was arrested and detained for two days. And then they deported them back to the Burma side—about six or seven women. After they were deported they came back. After that they made friends with the intelligence. We need to talk and give food to the police, sometimes money. I heard they also share information. They did this before they were arrested also.
Q: If you were already friends with the police why did everyone in the office get arrested?
We make friends to stay but we don't have complete guarantee, but it is better than nothing. (Respondent 2)

Establishing effective relationships with the authorities has been crucial to advancing the work of politically active women in the borderlands generally, and of women's political groups specifically. Without such relationships activism can be seriously curtailed, primarily through limitations on activists' movements due to their lack of legal status, or through unchecked exposure to other policing agencies likely to detain and deport activists. Individual women in this research testified to the importance of their organisation being able to negotiate these relationships, not only for themselves but also for individual activists whose situation is precarious because of their extra legal status:

> I don't feel scared or afraid when doing my work—because I have my organisation behind me. If I have some work to do and something happens my leader will negotiate with the police for me. (Respondent 5)

However, the relationships with state agencies are always complex: protection is not guaranteed and the relationships are unpredictable. Moreover, although the aims of political activists and Thai authorities may at times align, arrangements are always founded on the basis that these alignments are unstable and shaped by broader geopolitical arrangements between Thailand and Burma:

> I would like to explain my experience—some are good—and give support to the democracy movement. But the Thai Government they have an economic relationship with the Burmese Government that means they have a good relationship with the military and when military representatives come they welcome them. So I am not sure what role intelligence plays. One side they support us and on the other side they support the military. (Respondent 2)

6 Travel/Mobility

> We need to be very careful of ourselves. If we are arrested we cannot work and we cannot complain because we are illegal. (Respondent 2)

The women interviewed agreed that their access to travel documents depended on Thai policy and practices in the borderlands at any given time. The Thai Government is at different times more or less strict in its treatment of political groups working in the borderlands. Following high-profile security incidents security becomes tighter and access to Thai-issued travel documents more difficult.

> In the month of the Burmese embassy siege we needed to stay one month in the house and not go out—and security was tight. Security goes up and down, depending on the situation. (Respondent 2)

Women's groups working on the Thai–Burma border have in the past negotiated clearances to travel with intelligence via other organisations, namely those headed by men.

> Before we did not contact them directly, but now we do. They think that women can't do things. They don't like that. But now a little bit different, sometimes they call here on the phone. Now they contact us directly and want to know what is going on. Before women did not want to go near the intelligence, because they want to joke or have sex with the women.

However, simply because women received clearance from intelligence to travel and undertake political activities did not mean they had complete protection from being picked up by other agencies.

At the Constitution seminar, there were six to eight different intelligence groups who came to the seminar, even after security was supposedly arranged from Bangkok and three intelligence men came from Bangkok to watch over the conference. Even then there were rumours that ABSDF (All Burma Students' Democratic Front) women were in Chiang Mai and were going to set off bombs. At that time the news was from the SPDC, they made up the story that they were going to bomb, they were making rumours and putting them in the intelligence networks.

When travelling to town or undertaking other activities outside the compound or camp, these women seek to avoid arrest. Similar to migrant labourers they want to blend in and not come to the attention of local authorities. Women carefully observe and then imitate the styles of hair, clothes and even mannerisms of local Thai women, in order to be less conspicuous:

We should wear Thai-style clothes—make our hairstyles also to be like Thai style. Mae Hong Son is a rural area where people still dress in traditional clothes. We dress well when we travel or go to Chiang Mai or Bangkok. Even those with passports, Burmese passports are not a guarantee of safety because they know that they are not real ones. They can tear them up. (Respondent 4)

When travelling sometimes we wear Thai style and we just risk going without documents. But if we go to Bangkok we ask for travelling documents. By plane from Mae Hong Son to Chiang Mai is a little cheap. But we want to go to Bangkok we must go by bus because the flight is expensive. On the road to Bangkok there are many police checkpoints. Here in Bangkok we need to change our behaviour to make it the same as Thai people. We need to know how Thai girls wear their clothes and do like that when we go out. And we cut our hair. When we go out, we only speak English. We always say we are from the Philippines.

Different travel restrictions operate in different places, often dependent upon which agency effectively regulates travel or the changing political or operational priorities of the time. Moreover, travel restrictions are informed by the perception and experience of the authorities in relation to particular groups of women, specifically whether they are regarded as bona fide activist groups, migrants seeking work or other suspect groups:

I think Mae Hong Son and Chiang Mai is a little less difficult than Bangkok and Mae Sot— less difficult to negotiate with Thai authorities. The difference is because in Bangkok more people are there and the Thai authorities cannot know early who they are and what they do. In Mae Hong Son they can know who is the real political activist and who are not—they can know easily.

It is more difficult than before because the intelligence that used to give the documents that guarantee our safety no longer give documents and can no longer guarantee our safety. Not completely. Also from Sangkhlaburi and Bangkok the gates [on the roads], the checking points are increased. Now if we travel we take more risk. Or we take the police car. We negotiate with the police car and travel with the police in the high position in the province. We travel just with the police. (Respondent 2)

Even when women and their organisations are successful in negotiating effective relationships with authorities, this is not necessarily the case in the next area, town or city. Women's testimonies indicate that such relationships are a means of avoiding full contact with the criminal justice system, rather than freedom of movement:

> So the intelligence does not guarantee that we will get to our destination but it protects us from arrest. (Respondent 5)

Politically active women all noted that while they in no way felt safe or protected in a predictable or ongoing fashion by the authorities, they did identify the differences that came as a result of their negotiations with the authorities compared to other less-organised groups of women not directly associated with the democracy movement.

> In Burma it is dangerous, we could get raped by soldiers and forced to do forced labour. This exactly happens. In Thailand if we are lucky we can escape—if someone is arrested then others will collect money and negotiate and they will be released. I heard many stories of many women from Burma who are raped by Thai police—they are mostly migrant workers. I hear in Sangkhlaburi from many migrant workers who come to our office and we talk there. (Respondent 2)

Women who are able to obtain a level of, albeit precarious, recognition of their political activism by authorities, and hence usefulness in some measure to the Thai state, experience some limited advantage in a situation where their movement, work and lives remain seriously curtailed by their uncertain migration, social and legal status.

> Yes, for travelling and staying they can get some protection but for the ordinary women they have nothing and must do this themselves. And if they are arrested they don't know how to contact anyone and no one would realise what has happened to them. Women in the political organisations at least know how to get help from others. There are some networks and connections with the police already. Migrant women have nothing. Women in the refugee camps—for the wife if she wants to go shopping we can get a paper to go for a few days but the opportunity is little. And if we want to come out to attend training somewhere then we inform them at the gate and if the soldiers at the gate allow then we can go. For women inside the camp it is safer than outside the camp. Inside the camp at least we have our friends beside us, and if they treat us badly many people can easily see and be found out. Outside the camp nobody can help. (Respondent 2)

> When I went to attend counselling training in Mae Hong Son, on the way back the police caught me at the airport because I had no ID. They caught me in the waiting room—they came inside the waiting room and looked around for people who ducked their faces and avoided them. Then they went up and asked them for their ID card. I was shocked, and I said that I had no ID card and they asked me questions, and to show them document—what are you doing and where do you come from? They spoke Thai language. I told them I was a teacher and they were a little bit ashamed and talked to me better.

> They took me to the immigration office and asked me more questions—this time they spoke in Shan. They told me I was illegal and explained the law. But if I could pay money I could go. But then I called the [NGO] office but they said there was no one there at the time. I waited for nearly two hours and the immigration person could not wait any longer so they sent me to the police station. The police asked me the same questions that the immigration asked and then put me in prison…. One man came from [the NGO] went to the immigration office and said I was one of his people. At first the immigration officers did not want to let

me go, they wanted to complete their duty and send me to the border. They negotiated a long time and after that they let me go. (Respondent 3)

7   Sexual Violence

As Jan Carpenter (2006) has cogently argued in relation to the US–Mexico border, selective border enforcement mechanisms can be enacted in highly gendered ways while at the same time social control mechanisms within the home country operate against women in a similar fashion. Carpenter has argued that violent methods of social control used against women on the Mexican side of the border "...mirror the violence of United States border control policies and technologies of enforcement" (2006, pp. 167–168). Her research has identified the ways in which the increased militarisation of the border, through enhanced cooperation between the military and civilian law enforcement, has been based on the introduction and integration of military units in the border region and that border patrol has been modified to resemble the military in its infrastructure and operation. Falcon (2001) has documented the increased incidence of rape along the US–Mexico border, and argued that it has been a systematic and militarised use of rape. It has also been compared to rape utilised in conflict zones such as Rwanda and Bosnia. Carpenter has suggested that rape has not only been adopted as part of a broader project of border warfare, but also as a "price" for entry into the United States. Luibheid (2002) has detailed how the precarious legal status of women crossing borders has usually rendered responses to rape committed by state agents (and others) inept, if they exist at all. For the women interviewed in this research, the threat of sexual violence at the hands of state officials was always at the front of their minds when they came into unpredicted contact with the authorities on the Thai–Burma border:

> I stayed in the police jail two nights and three days. They were men guards that looked after us. They looked down on us because we were women and illegal and young. I heard that in this situation young women could be raped. So I told them I was a teacher and I came to teach and wanted to go to Chiang Mai. Mostly they ignored me out the back. They don't search or touch me. But they shouted and intimidated me. I was worried that they might do something to me. I did not sleep the whole night. The Thai police, I heard can do things to people from Burma. So I did not sleep—I walked and sat down. I was alone in the cell. (Respondent 3)

Women activists know that the Thai authorities can assault and rape with virtual impunity, and that contact with the Thai authorities is not always directly in relation to their political activities and therefore is not always politically negotiable. Although these women occupy a relatively privileged position, their race and gender still restrict them to an easily excludable population. As Luibheid has argued, borders are not only marked as lines on maps but are played out in social, racial and gendered contests which are often violent and often played out on the bodies of individuals. Women have developed a variety of strategies and networks to help avoid arrest, yet no measure is guaranteed, and there are gaps that expose their acute vulnerability including being pulled up by Thai authorities and making contact with their own people who can help. At these moments, women's confidence is crucial to their personal safety. One activist described the following experience:

> Once I was on the way back to Mae Sariang I had immigration pass but the police pulled me off the bus—me and my daughter. When they arrested me I asked to phone BWU and they made arrangements. At that time I was really scared because they took me and my daughter—I don't know where—they took my wallet and asked me questions. I snapped, "Why did you take that?" I felt scared, my daughter was scared. But even though I was scared I answered them back. There were three police. I was scared because I had heard often that Burmese women in prisons were abused. I thought that when they pulled me off the bus they would take me to the police station. If they had taken me to the police station then I would not be scared. But they took us by car into a jungle place. (Respondent 5)

> Mothers travel more easily because they bring their children because security don't want to take care of the children or be responsible for that situation. So normally they don't bother mothers. (Respondent 6)

8   Policing the Borderland

As a result of the contested and limbo-like nature of this space, the policing of the Thai–Burma border is contradictory for women who live and work in the borderland. The policing of people coming across the border and the consequences of their very presence in Thailand are highly complex. The border space is regulated or policed by immigration, police and intelligence agencies, all of whom have different mandates but perform policing-type functions in relation to the people living in or transiting this area. The presence, movement and meetings of the politically active women with whom I was working are of concern to the Thai authorities in the context of the diverse, shifting and unpredictable social, military and political landscape of the borderlands. They are of course also of interest to the Burmese regime.

The policing that politically active women have experienced in the borderlands highlights the plurality of and disharmony among the different branches of the security forces that all contribute to the broader border policing project: police, intelligence, army and immigration agencies. Despite these practices women find space to move, literally. Sometimes politically active women are differentiated by Thai authorities as either refugees or migrants, at other times not. The ambiguity arising here also provides women with opportunities to move in ways that would otherwise be prevented, but at the same time does not insure them against danger.

When women are arrested or detained for their illegal status they are forced to negotiate in the shadow of actual or threatened sexual violence and shame. In short, the fear of sexual violence constantly intersects with (at best) a clouded and precarious relationship with the Thai state.

Women's accounts of border policing demonstrate the gendered ways in which border points are enforced by state agencies (as borders), and the gendered ways women need to negotiate these border points. These stories also illuminate the fiction of the "border" through women negotiating them—for example, by walking around border points and avoiding authorities. In the women's minds are destinations, not borders and nation-states—although the latter still inform women's activism at other levels. State practices of enforcing territorial state boundaries can be destabilised by focusing on women's experiences of policing, which contradict meta-narratives of discrete, (assumedly) demarcated, fixed boundaries between two countries. Women's accounts illustrate how states may intentionally rely on practising the maintenance of "flexible" boundaries. The borderland is an ambivalent space—a space of political activism and a potential space of refuge, and also a space of unchecked violence and unpredictable regulation and control by state agencies.

Borders have been considered by some theorists as imaginary lines on the surface of the earth (McCorquodale, 2001). For those areas that we may regard as borderlands or frontiers, the idea or imaginary of the border is constantly produced and reproduced by the policing of transversal subjects. Women who have fled Burma and who participate in the democracy movement along the Thai–Burma border remain between law and conflict, negotiating the violence and threat of violence between their home and host country in surprisingly ordinary and everyday ways. The transversal space between law and conflict in the borderland at times requires careful negotiation, yet at others it is far more combative. The policing of politically active women's lives on the Thai–Burma border has been imprecise, constantly moving and transforming dependent on a range of conditions. So too have women's responses—which are at times uncompromising, at others uncertain, yet always strategic.

9   Summary

The Thai–Burma border is a complex site to understand the development of a frontier that is at once a borderland as well as an integrated part of both sending country (Burma) and receiving country (Thailand). The Thai–Burma border presents a recognisable borderland where border crossings last lifetimes. Interviews with politically active women living and working in the borderland evidence the need to expand narrow conceptions of border policing to consider the complex relationships and policing practices that exert control and facilitate movement in these peculiar spaces. This chapter focuses on a particular group of women: those who have overtly engaged in political processes for democracy in Burma, including women active in the Bamar, Karen, Kachin and Shan communities. In this regard, this is no ordinary group of women, as they have crossed a border and live in compromised circumstances, and include women who have been active in carving out a space for women's political voices to be heard and are daily involved in improving their communities.

Chapter 4
A Gate at the Border?

Asylum and Gender-Based Persecution

*The question of whether or not the appellants have refugee
status is of theoretical importance to the appellants. They have
been given leave to enter the United Kingdom because article
3 of the European Convention on Human Rights forbids their
return to their home countries for so long as they are at risk
of torture or inhuman or degrading treatment or punishment
there. So far so good. But leave to enter does not give them a
right to remain in this country. If their claims for asylum are
recognised, however, all the benefits of the Refugee Convention
will then be available to them. The uncertainty that attaches to
their present lack of status will be replaced by the status which
the Contracting States have undertaken to accord to a refugee
and by all the rights that attach to it. This is a very substantial
additional benefit which is well worth arguing for.*

(Lord Hope of Craighead at 35 on Fornah)

1 Getting to the Gate

Ms Kasinga arrived by plane in the United States in 1994. She had fled Togo where
she had been forced into marriage and was about to be forced to undergo female
genital mutilation (FGM). Her sister gave her money to buy the aeroplane ticket and
she left the family home while the head of the household was out. Her sister drove
her to the airport in Accra, Ghana and she took the first plane out—to Germany.
According to reports of the case, Ms Kasinga lived in Dusseldorf for two months
under an arrangement that she would cook and clean in exchange for board. She
bought a passport from a man who advised her to go to the United States where she
had a cousin and where she could make a claim for asylum. When she arrived in the
United States at Newark Airport in December 1994 she immediately told the customs officer that she had travelled on a false passport and wanted to claim asylum.

Ms Kasinga was taken to the Esmor Detention Centre. Ms Kasinga had no criminal record and had a relative in the United States willing to support her. Reports
have described the abuses and indignities she suffered while in Esmor:

S. Pickering, *Women, Borders, and Violence,*
DOI 10.1007/978-1-4419-0271-9_4, © Springer Science+Business Media, LLC 2011

...she was put in a large cold room with no windows except for a small one in the metal door. A guard told her to take off her clothes. It was the first time Ms Kasinga, then 17 years old, had undressed in front of a stranger. She was menstruating and asked to keep her underwear, but she said the guard refused. Freezing and scared, she sat on a toilet in the room, shivering. When she looked up at one point, she saw a male guard looking at her through the door. The humiliations of life at Esmor, a jail that was privately run under a contract with the immigration service, had only begun. She was given a pair of sandals, both for the right foot, and stained underwear that fell down unless she tucked it under a belt. At one point, she was put in a small isolation cell for five days because she washed her hands before sunrise in a ritual before her morning prayers, breaking a rule that no one was to use the showers before 6 a.m. (Lewis, 1996, *The New York Times*)

Ms Kasinga was inside Esmor Detention Centre when a riot broke out on 18 June 2005. During the riot Ms Kasinga was tear gassed and beaten. An Immigration and Naturalization Service (INS) report into the incident found that Esmor, a privately contracted centre, was found to be in breach of its contractual obligations with the INS, particularly concerning accountability and oversight of Centre personnel, in real terms had manifest in the routine abuse and harassment of detainees, poorly trained guards who beat detainees. The report found that the guards had treated detainees with "capricious cruelty". Lawyers and human rights advocates had complained about conditions in Esmor for years. The Centre detained people whose asylum claims had been in process for extended periods, some for many years. Asylum seekers were suffering physically and psychologically from the harsh conditions. The INS allowed its contract with Esmor to lapse. The riot against the conditions in Esmor was subject to many commentaries and eventually a report which was scathing of the Centre. The Esmor report, while highly critical of the violence and cruelty of particular detention centre staff, also identified a core driver of the abuse as the asylum system itself: a system which routinely found those detained to be bona fide refugees, like Ms Kasinga. After the riot in Esmor, Ms Kasinga was transferred to two prisons in Pennsylvania where she was strip searched and locked in a maximum security cell she had to share with a convicted prisoner. Ms Kasinga was only released following the campaign of her legal advocates in the media, including a campaign by *The New York Times*.

The *Kasinga* case, and the violence and abuses in Esmor, took place during a period when the United States was transitioning from a policy of avoiding immigration detention for asylum seekers towards heightened border protection and enforcement fuelled by increased national security concerns. The Esmor abuses were a precursor to what later took place at other immigration detention facilities, including at Krome in Florida where a guard was charged with sexual assault and investigations found evidence of widespread abuse of female detainees (Stop Prisoner Rape, 2004). A series of investigations have raised serious concerns over practices of sexual abuse in immigration detention centres in the United States, including the lack of independent monitoring of detainee conditions (Stop Prisoner Rape, 2004) and inadequate healthcare in immigration detention (Human Rights Watch, 2009c). The effect of the investigations was that the United States embraced the routine use of detention of asylum seekers, which was considered an important part of deterring bogus applicants. The *Illegal Immigration Reform and Immigrant Responsibility*

Act (1996) included a range of restrictions to impede the ability of refugees to gain protection in the United States, including expedited removal (which gave INS officials at airports and borders the power to order immediate deportation of people who arrived in the United States without proper travel documents), the mandatory detention of all asylum seekers who are subject to expedited removal (with limited parole possibilities), and the one-year filing deadline (which prevents asylum claims that are not made within one year of arrival in the United States). It is impossible to determine how many refugees failed to access refugee determination processes and potential protection because of these laws (Lawyers Committee for Human Rights, 2002). It is also impossible to identify with accuracy how these laws might have impacted women differently to men. However, there can be no doubt that women are particularly vulnerable to strategies such as expedited removal, highlighted by the extant literature which demonstrates that women are seldom ready to disclose often humiliating details of gendered sexual assault during their first contact with host country officials. In addition, it is widely recognised that survivors of torture and trauma are often unable to talk about what has happened to them, particularly on demand or under threat of removal. The mandatory detention of asylum seekers has seen parole applied in a discretionary manner once asylum seekers establish that they have a credible claim. Women have testified to the impact of submitting to prison-like regimes during detention, which include wearing culturally foreign uniforms and a lack of privacy, and the deleterious physical and psychological effects of imprisonment on those who have fled persecution, including being separated from their children. In the aftermath of 9/11, changes to the Board of Immigration Appeals (BIA) led some human rights groups to suggest that the Board had simply become a mechanism for rubber-stamping the decisions of INS officials (Lawyers Committee for Human Rights, 2002). The US Lawyers Committee for Human Rights has argued that preventing women from applying for asylum on procedural grounds or when they are detained under inhumane conditions undermines advancements in legal jurisprudence that recognise gender-based persecution.

In 1998, Zaineb Fornah and her mother were living in her father's family village to escape the civil war when she overheard discussions of her impending subjection to FGM. Ms Fornah was not willing to undergo FGM and ran away but was soon captured by rebels and repeatedly raped by a rebel leader, to whom she became pregnant. Her uncle arranged her flight from Sierra Leone to the UK. She later claimed that if she returned to Sierra Leone she would have nowhere to live but her father's village, where she feared she would be subjected to FGM. She reached the United Kingdom at the age of 15 with the help of her uncle who resided in the United States, and was cared for by the West Sussex Social Services Child Asylum Team. She largely relied on pro bono legal services to advance her legal case.

The cases, like that of Kasinga above, discussed further on in this chapter are illustrative rather than definitive. That is because the determinations to grant women asylum in these stories were fought for long and hard and were successful, but ultimately did not provide predictable legal practices in granting women a legal (refugee-based) exception at the border. I consider the cases of Kasinga and Fornah to be a lens through which to understand how crossing borders increasingly involves not only the journey to the border, but also women's legal negotiation to be recognised and granted a privileged status among peoples forced to migrate: to be given the legal status of refugee. The experience of border crossing undertaken by women seeking asylum requires us to better understand the nature of the gate in the border fence, in particular how refugee determination processes make sense of gender-based persecution.

Refugee status can be seen as a gate in the increasingly impregnable legal fence that excludes unwanted populations from the Global North. It is a narrow gate, and in many places getting narrower every year. A gender analysis of refugee determination shows that this gate is shut to large numbers of women who experience sexual violence, despite overwhelming evidence that gender-based persecution is increasing globally. The analysis of legal arguments and refugee determination processes reveals the power of discourse in legitimising women's unauthorised border crossings into the Global North, and by extension the problematic consequences of border policing which militate against global mobility in blanket and all-consuming ways. The gate of refugee protection is well worth prising open, for it ordinarily comes with a stable migration status for women and their families. As Lord Hope of Craighead says above, the benefit is well worth arguing for.

2   Arriving at Asylum

When asylum seekers arrive at the physical borders of the nation-state, they are invariably subject to regimes of reception, detention or rejection, often elaborate inter-agency policing arrangements among immigration agencies, and military and civilian policing. Countries of the Global North that are signatories to the Refugee Convention are obliged to accept those people who make a claim for asylum from immediate deportation. In such cases the border policing edifice is transformed to accommodate individuals who seek to make a legal claim against being immediately policed out of the nation-state. These countries are meant to "open the gate" for the period of time required to undertake a legal process to determine whether the claimant is owed refugee protection. Such "transformation" may initially mean little more than the failure of the state to turn a boat back or to immediately deport the person in question, instead subjecting them to detention within large institutions or the community, or to periods of extended uncertainty regarding their migration status, until such time as their asylum claim is concluded. Often, even then, their status can result in a subsidiary form of protection that may be temporary and entail limited benefits and supports. Moreover, there is a growing body of evidence of a global trend among wealthy states of adopting a range of formal and informal legal and operational strategies to avoid the legal obligations of the Refugee Convention, particularly in relation to those who cross borders claiming they are fleeing from gender-based persecution. When an asylum claim is made, a legal determination of the claim is routinely undertaken. Despite increasing efforts to limit the legal avenues available to pursue refugee status and thereby take a place within a privileged group of the world's stateless peoples, such avenues remain a point of leverage against the almost total border policing effort against unwanted populations. Therefore, it is important to consider what happens when gender-based claims form the basis for trying to keep the gate wedged open.

In considering refugee claim determinations and gender-based persecution it is necessary to acknowledge that this (problematic) gate in the fence is available only to those women who are able to reach nations that have signed the Convention. Overwhelmingly, it is much more difficult for women to reach the borders of the Global South than it is for their male counterparts.

Migration holds more dangers for women—notably during the journey, when they may experience physical, sexual or other forms of abuse. Travelling to a border is in itself a physical endurance test, in which women are at a social, cultural and physical disadvantage. Single women and girls are particularly at risk (UNHCR, 2007b, Statistical Yearbook). Women and girls represent on average 47% of persons of concern to UNHCR, and 44% of refugees and asylum seekers are children below 18 years of age (UNHCR, 2008 global trends). Gender has proved to be a difficulty for those charged with managing and supporting refugees worldwide. It is not since 2001 that UNHCR has published robust statistical profiles that include gender in sufficient detail to be meaningful. Even then, they noted the difficulty of generating information regarding gender, including the seemingly anomalous situation that the gender breakdown for refugees in the developing world was far better reported than for the developed world (UNHCR, 2001). Despite women being in need of protection in almost equal numbers to men, we know that fewer arrive in the Global North and that this is often because of the factors that militate against their mobility.

3 The Refugee Definition: Gender and Particular Social Group (PSG)

> Owing to a well-founded fear of being persecuted for reasons of race, religion, nationality, membership of a particular social group or political opinion, is outside [her] country of origin and is unable or, owing to such fear, is unwilling to avail [herself] of the protection of that country; or who, not having nationality and being outside the country of [her] former habitual residence as a result of such events, is unable or, owing to such fear, is unwilling to return to it. (United Nations Refugee Convention, Article1(A)(2) 1951)

Drawn from the 1951 United Nations *Convention Relating to the Status of Refugees*, Article 1(A)(2) constitutes the international legal definition of a refugee. The definition utilises a particularly rigid understanding of persecution in which gender is not an enumerated ground. Refugee applications made by women for reasons of gender-based persecution therefore need to "creatively" fit within one of the five enumerated grounds. In some countries gender has come to be interpreted domestically as falling within what it terms a "particular social group" (for example, gender was recognised as grounds for PSG in the 1997 Canadian Supreme Court case *Canada (Attorney General) v Ward* (2 SCR 689, INLR 42)). In 2002, the High

Court of Australia found for an applicant in a case of gender-based persecution (domestic violence) using the Convention's ground "particular social group" (Cauchi, 2002). The Australian case of *Minister for Immigration and Multicultural Affairs v Khawar* (HCA 14 2002) centred on the issue of the circumstances in which women are entitled to international protection where the persecution is perpetrated by non-state actors. This case resulted in a landmark decision in as much as the highest court in the land determined that women are entitled to state protection from domestic violence. The Australian Refugee Review Tribunal (RRT) had rejected the woman's claim because it considered domestic violence to be a "personal dispute" and not within the purview of Australia's refugee obligations. In not being accorded police protection, Mrs Khawar successfully argued that the Pakistani law was being applied in a discriminatory fashion. The High Court determined that a nexus could be found between (gender-based) persecution and a stipulated Convention ground (i.e. "particular social group") regardless of whether the abuse was committed by state or non-state actors. Whether the Australian Parliament will legislate against this decision in relation to gender is unclear. However, it is important to remember that the cases analysed in this study took place prior to the decision outlined above.

Some feminists have called for the addition of gender as the sixth prohibited ground for persecution (Greatbatch, 1989). However, other feminists have suggested that women's experiences of persecution are ignored because the key criteria for being a refugee are drawn primarily from the realm of public sphere activities which are traditionally undertaken in many societies by men (Indra, 1987). The addition of "gender" as an enumerated ground for refugee status would do little to improve the position of refugee women without a redefinition of "persecution" that gives credibility to women's private sphere experiences. Moreover, the inclusion of gender as a ground for refugee status assumes consensus on the nature of gender-based persecution (Greatbatch, 1989).

This chapter considers recent developments in refugee jurisprudence in a number of countries that have developed new, or newly clarified, routes for women's legal recognition as refugees and looks also at the ways they can be easily undermined. It considers recent jurisprudential developments in relation to female genital cutting (FGC), the discursive manoeuvres adopted to keep women's claims from being considered legitimate under the provisions of the Refugee Convention, and legitimate reasons to keep the gate open. It concludes by arguing that refugee determination continues to be an unstable vehicle for women seeking protection, and produces curious outcomes for policing women both inside and outside borders.

4 The Gate in Operation

Barsky (1994) has offered a compelling account of hegemonic readings of the refugee. In drawing on the writings of Bourdieu and Bahktin as well as Foucault, Barsky studied the transcripts of refugee applications in Canada. Importantly, he produced a framework for considering how transcripts effectively produce the "Other":

First, it should demonstrate the degree to which the "Other" can be constructed through discourse, and the ways in which this construction can be productive towards a pre-determined end; second, it should emphasize the institutional aspects of language and the ways that particular examples of discursive practices are infused with the social structure within which they occur; and third, it should unveil the ways in which discursive practice further legitimizes the socio-political structures which it expresses and (therefore) helps to reproduce. (Barsky, 1994, p. 3)

The Other who emerges from the transcriptions of the refugee determination process is "diminished to the point of near non-existence" (Barsky, 1994, p. 4). The alleged neutrality of the refugee definition is read through a series of legal arguments and signs related to the crucial issue of refugee status to reveal that every element of the definition remains imprecise. Moreover, the language of the process is multiply interpreted through both translation and culture. In short, the vagaries of the definition of "refugee" transpose experiences of persecution into abstracted interpretations of legal discourse (cf. Conklin, 1997). Knowing of the persecution is not to know expertly of the legal discourse that comes to disembody persecution within the determination process.

A study of Australian RRT decisions may similarly reveal the operation of language in relation to human suffering and the role of the nation-state in distancing and denying suffering in the administrative legal realm. In his influential work *States of Denial,* Cohen outlined the multifarious ways in which individuals, groups and states come to deny suffering and atrocities (Cohen, 2001). For benign, neutral or malignant reasons "our cumulative knowledge of recent or current atrocities is incomplete, uneven and unobjective" (Cohen, 2001, p. 101). Official discourses of denial, as identified by Cohen, can take a number of forms. *Literal denial* often relies on attacking the reliability and credibility of the observer. *Interpretive denial* often uses euphemisms to "mark, sanitize or confer respectability" on events whereby "palliative terms deny or misrepresent cruelty or harm, giving them neutral or respectable status" (Cohen, 2001, p. 107). *Legalistic denial* draws from the language of legality itself that "results in the intricate textual commentaries that circulate between governments and their critics or within legal-diplomatic loops and UN committees" (Cohen, 2001, p. 107). *Denial of responsibility* entails an acknowledgement that something bad happened but that the official body in question is not responsible.

These four kinds of denial identified by Cohen are traced in the RRT decisions under study here. In particular, how do approaches to the enumerated ground of "particular social group" use discourses of denial? In what ways does its denial see gender-based persecution normalised and naturalised? This research will examine what Cohen describes as the "accounts and rhetorical devices" that include active ideological justifications that deny suffering (Cohen, 2001, p. 59). In short, what gendered ideological justifications are provided that deny gender-based suffering, and what impact does this have on women's attempts to gain refugee protection from developed nations?

An RRT decision is presented as a stylised document that usually covers the following areas: background; the law; claims and evidence; findings and reasons;

conclusion; and decision. It does so utilising a legalistic language and slips between usage of the first and third person. It also shifts from quoting a woman's testimony to rewording that testimony (or between direct discourse and indirect discourse: see Fairclough, 1998, p. 56). It refers to the woman as the "applicant" and regulates the text with phrases such as "it was alleged" and "the applicant suggested". An RRT decision includes extended references to relevant, and sometimes irrelevant, case law. Overall it is a read-alone document that represents the singular legal approach of the RRT member and his or her decisions to include and exclude certain parts of the woman's application as deemed appropriate. The reported testimony of the woman is usually only referred to in relation to the veracity of the evidence and the ability of the RRT to source "established" and "reliable" sources—such as the US State Department—to confirm her story. In so doing, the RRT often shatters the woman's story into indiscernible pieces. She thus suffers the mistreatment of not having her story recorded in a coherent fashion, and her story becomes but a weave in the monologue of the Tribunal member speaking in legal language, her utterances nameless and adrift within that monologue. Even if the woman accepts, or attempts to enter, the legal discourse of the proceedings she is disembodied and without voice in the record of those proceedings. The prioritisation of legal discourse in refugee determination ensures that the vocabulary of the refugee definition will continue to approximate the neutrality of a human rights code, which at the same time reinforces the power of the nation-state to include and exclude. The RRT decision is a monologue of international law embodied in a domestic legal document. It is a monologue of refugeehood, about the nation, about gender, but rarely about the persecution experienced by the woman before it.

The reading offered here pays particular attention to the use of gendered and cultural stereotypes to simultaneously undermine gender-based persecution and "particular social group" in cases before the RRT. This chapter utilises case analysis in order to offer a detailed reading of the narration of cases involving gender-based persecution and the so-called "particular social group". Such a critical reading seeks to examine the nuanced ways in which hostility is expressed in RRT decisions.

In examining how gender has been talked about when "particular social group" is the basis of women's appeals to the RRT, 25 cases were investigated in depth. The sample was heavily weighted for decisions that were successful[1] (set aside) on "particular social group" grounds so that we could undertake a more detailed examination of the hostile interpretation of "particular social group" in cases of gender-based persecution (see Tables 4.1 and 4.2).[2]

---

[1] In RRT decisions an appeal is successful when the original decision (which found that the applicant was not a refugee) is referred to as "set aside" (i.e. the RRT finds that the applicant is a refugee) and unsuccessful when it is referred to as "affirmed" (i.e. the RRT agrees with the original decision that the applicant is not a refugee).

[2] I found that there were many more cases set aside that were based on both "particular social group" and political opinion. I have included some of these in this study. Of the 25 cases considered, 14 were set aside and the remaining 11 were affirmed.

Table 4.1 Cases studied

Cases	Number of cases	Country of origin
Set aside (appeal successful)	14	3 Philippines, 1 Bangladesh, 1 Lebanon, 2 Iran, 1 Ukraine, 1 Nigeria, 1 Chile, 1 Turkey, 1 Albania, 2 Somalia
Affirmed (appeal unsuccessful)	11	2 Lebanon, 2 China, 1 Ghana, 1 Somalia, 1 Bolivia, 1 Thailand, 1 Poland

Table 4.2 Convention grounds used and their outcomes

Convention grounds	Number of cases	Set aside/affirmed
Particular social group	14	8 set aside
Particular social group and political opinion	8	4 set aside
Political opinion	1	Set aside
Particular social group, political opinion and religion	1	Set aside
Particular social group, nationality or origin	1	Affirmed

In these 25 cases if "particular social group" was used, it was most successful when coupled with another ground. This suggests that "particular social group" in relation to gender-based persecution remains relatively underdeveloped as a legal ground in its own right. However, for many gender-related persecution claims there remains no other recourse of action. Consequently, it remains a ground upon which recognition of many forms of gender-based persecution are precariously positioned. Furthermore, when "particular social group" is used it is most successful in conjunction with other human rights instruments, particularly the *Universal Declaration of Human Rights* and the *International Covenant on Civil and Political Rights,* and to a more limited extent the *Convention Against Torture, and Other Cruel, Inhuman and Degrading Treatment or Punishment,* and the *Convention on the Elimination of all Forms of Discrimination Against Women.*

5   The Story of Five Cases

5.1   *Case 1*

The first case was made by a Lebanese woman (RRT 1995, N95/07492). The case was set aside. The case concerned a woman subjected to sexual harassment and assault by Syrian soldiers in her border village. The woman applied for refugee status both on the basis of political opinion and the ground of "particular social group". In this case the RRT made the following general finding in relation to "particular social group": "Women are an example of a social group which exists across all countries and societies and whose membership involves millions" (RRT 1995, N95/07492, 8).

The RRT went on to make the following series of comments incoming to the final decision to set the case aside:

> Despite the fact that there is much evidence that women in Lebanon suffer from discrimination which in some cases can be severe, the applicant herself has experienced this no more than any other woman. In fact the applicant has been better positioned than other women from her country. She has been allowed to operate her own business and has been granted great freedom of movement. (RRT 1995, N95/07492, 28)

> As for the harassment she experienced at the hands of the Syrian soldier, distressing though this may have been to the applicant, this treatment falls short of the harm envisaged by the term persecution under the Convention. People have infatuations for others for a variety of reasons and can cause them great distress as a result. Unfortunately for the applicant in the present case, he chose as the object of his interest the applicant herself. (RRT 1995, N95/07492, 28)

> As for the applicant's claim that she suffered harassment at the hands of a Syrian soldier, the Tribunal does not believe the harm she experienced (being pestered and followed by him) amounts to persecution. (RRT 1995, N95/07492, 28)

> Also the evidence also [sic] cited above shows that the Syrian army is now rather better behaved than they were several years ago when the applicant departed Lebanon. (RRT 1995, N95/07492, 28)

The RRT was of the opinion that the woman had not experienced persecution more than had anyone else within the particular social group broadly defined by this RRT member (the fact that her greater freedom of movement may put her at greater risk than other women in terms of increased contact with Syrian soldiers was not canvassed). In this case, a wide definition of "particular social group" makes possible the diminution of persecution in highly gendered ways. This was most evident in the choice of vocabulary used by the RRT member: "distressing", "infatuations", "unfortunate", "chose", "object of his interest" and "pestered". The assumption is that the applicant is acted upon and can only reasonably expect to be acted upon (it is "unfortunate", "he [chooses] his interest", she remains "the object"). Such terminology also interpretively denies the gender-based persecution by misrepresenting her experiences as ordinary relations between the sexes.

Rather than tackle the thorny issue of "particular social group" and gender, the RRT settles on a broad definition of "particular social group" and then pursues this pointed and belittling commentary to evade "particular social group" grounds. The language selected empties the broad "particular social group" definition of all its effective content. In addition, such commentary can only be put forward under the ideological condition that women cannot be marginalised in a global sense in all societies or even in a global sense in any one society. What does "better behaved" Syrian soldiers mean for the woman before the RRT?

The suffering of the woman was acknowledged by the RRT but responsibility for redressing it was denied. Gender-based persecution becomes suffering because it is considered not the kind of persecution envisaged by the Convention. As a result, suffering is reducible to "distress" as a result of "infatuations". Gender-based persecution therefore does not need to be named and was neatly placed beyond the purview of international refugee protection and the RRT.

The RRT proceeded to set aside the original decision on the basis of the woman's claim regarding political opinion and being targeted because of her political associations. In doing so, the RRT is not restricted in how it narrates gender and "particular social group". In fact, when the RRT leaves the serious business of refugee determination to the grounds of political opinion it is then able to talk fast and loose about gender as it is considered peripheral to the serious business of political opinion and persecution, and hence grounds for refugee status.

5.2 Case 2

The second case examined was made by an Iranian woman who had refused to submit to the severity of the Islamic code as enforced by the Government of Iran (RRT 1995, N95/09580). Her application, made on the basis of "particular social group" and political opinion, was set aside. The narrative offered by the RRT outlined a case based on the woman being forced into an arranged marriage in which she was severely beaten, raped and threatened with disfigurement. The woman attempted to live apart from her husband but went back because her children were with her husband. She began an affair, which was against religious law. When the affair with the man ended, he passed on information about her which was then used by a third man to blackmail her. When she fled to Australia she received documents sentencing her to stoning.

The woman based her "particular social group" status on "women who have committed adultery", but the RRT morphed this into "Iranian woman who had refused to submit to the severity of the Islamic code as it is enforced by the government" (RRT 1995, N95/09580, 4). The RRT argued that her membership of a "particular social group" was:

> …proved by the fact that the state also defined women who did not adhere to social norms as being a particular "social group". They have been referred to by the state as being corrupt, seditious, dangerous and destructive to public honor and chastity, terrorists and prostitutes. (RRT 1995, N95/09580, 23)

The original decision-maker had found that the evidence in relation to the woman's extra-marital affair was not credible. "The decision maker also found it implausible that, in a country where the punishment for adultery was severe, the Applicant would have allowed evidence against her to be obtained as she claimed" (RRT 1995, N95/09580, 16). Such interpretive denial renders the woman naive, immature and a liar. However, in disputing the original decision-maker's characterisation, the RRT offers an equally problematic version of events that positions the applicant as part of a "particular social group" that can be characterised as emotional and irrational:

> In my view people do not always act rationally and in their own best interests at all times. I therefore consider that there are valid reasons why a woman with the Applicant's history might be drawn through naivity or desperation into a potentially dangerous relationship, and why in these circumstances she might not be as observant as others. (RRT 1995, N95/09580, 16)

In this case the definition of "particular social group" comes to constitute political opinion, which was more developed in the decision. The use of political opinion was made on the basis of the woman's rejection of Iranian religious and cultural norms as a political act (as well as constituting a "particular social group"). This may be considered a positive shift in the narration that clearly links gendered social norms to a concept of politics. However, the RRT did not believe that the applicant "overtly expresses any political opinion", but did find that the act of adultery was "interpreted as a political act and that this was a significant factor in contributing to the decision of the Iranian state to execute her" (RRT 1995, N95/09580, 24). The RRT considered an example of an overt act to be "the unwillingness of an Iranian woman to wear the chador and attend Islamic functions" (RRT 1995, N95/09580, 24). However, refusing to wear the chador is simply not an option for many women. Simplistic assertions regarding overt political actions are often based on the cultural assumptions of the decision-maker as to what is or is not overt or what should be considered overt.

The argument that the woman's act of adultery was not "overtly political" is contentious. The RRT transcript reflects that a political opinion within the private domain is not overtly political, whereas the public wearing of particular items or the non-attendance at functions is deemed to be overtly political. Such a distinction comes into crisis when the RRT says that the state accused women who reject the social norms of Iranian society as "instrumental in the foreign-inspired plot to undermine revolutionary Puritanism" (RRT 1995, N95/09580, 23). Similar to significant scholarship in the area (Crawley, 2001), this statement by the RRT member does not reflect the distinction between the public and private realms that the RRT, for the most part, has deployed in previous matters.

Moreover, the narration ignores significant work undertaken by feminist activists and scholars in highlighting the danger of a public–private distinction for women attempting to access justice (Charlesworth & Chinkin, 2000). In short, women in domestic criminal justice systems, civil legal systems and international legal systems have fought against the routine downgrading of their claims for justice, and misconceptions that the incident or issue they experienced lies outside the purview of public law and therefore should be left as a matter for the private individual or family realm. The mobilisation of these kinds of distinctions again sees refugee determination systems interpreting the refugee definition through the lens of predominantly male experiences of the public sphere and hence public (male) persecution.

The narration is not, however, limited to the gendered deployment of the public–private distinction. In adopting this distinction the narration is manoeuvring the woman away from the political heart of refugee status. One of the ways in which this is made further possible is through the coupling of gendered ideologies and cultural ideologies. In this case, a woman needed to embrace one of the most potent symbols of Islam for those in the West to consider her to have a political opinion: wearing a veil. Thus, the politics of veiling continues to paralyse the thinking of decision-makers. An appreciation of the politics of veiling is to be lauded. However, to singularly position physical and public symbolism as an example of political opinion is to decouple the very argument that led to such an acknowledgement of the politics of veiling: that is, that a woman's body, whether seen or unseen in public, can be considered a political matter relevant to establishing political opinion according to the terms of the Refugee Convention. Moreover, this approach means that the only political act in relation to veiling is the refusal to wear it, even though many Iranian women chose to veil at the time of the revolution in Iran as a political act (Macleod, 1995).

5.3   Case 3

The third case studied was made by a Lebanese woman on the basis of "particular social group" (RRT 1995, N95/09841), in which the RRT affirmed the decision. The RRT found the applicant had been widowed at a relatively young age and would have to live according to the standards deemed appropriate for a widow in Lebanese society, which meant she would be "denied personal freedom and denied all opportunities. She maintained that she is a human being who had the right to live as a human being, not according to the dictates of other people" (RRT 1995, N95/09841, 12).

The passivity of gender in relation to the construction of "particular social group" in this case was overwhelming. The RRT recognised "women are a particular social group for the purposes of the treaty" (RRT 1995, N95/09841, 18) and went on to affirm that widows may also be considered a "cognisable" social group:

> …they are generally of a certain age group, they are made to wear black and they must live according to the customs and in a manner which is deemed appropriate. They could be said to thus form a social group within a social group. However, as said above, the role is merely one part of the whole role allotted to women and so in essence cannot be separated from the general experience of women in Lebanon per se. It is simply that a woman at some stage in her life (if her husband should die before her) is expected to take on the role expected of a woman who is widowed—as a woman she could expect no more. (RRT 1995, N95/09841, 19)

The RRT did not accept that the woman was being discriminated against as a woman in her community or as a woman generally. Moreover, it suggested that traditional social mores cannot, realistically, be surmounted. Socially and culturally constructed meaning cannot be challenged by the woman, or for that matter by the RRT. On this view, such meanings remain static and innate characteristics of the woman's condition and, indeed, the condition of all women in this context.

The transcript positions the Tribunal member's worldview as "fact". These "facts" (such as the woman "can expect no more") depend upon a series of debilitatingly passive gender presumptions that are developed as the narration proceeds, which further reinforce the worldview of the RRT member and draw on forms of interpretive and legal denial:

> A mere accident of birth thus determines for life the role and position which a person will take according to their gender. There is no doubt that the discrimination a woman must face extends into almost every area of life in some form or another. She may be able to limit it to a great degree, but socially and culturally she can never be free of it. (RRT 1995, N95/09841, 18)

This narration of gender is the scaffolding upon which the RRT member builds the facts. The passivity of gender and the insurmountability of gendered social mores become a mutually reinforcing discourse. However, to view this meshing of discourses in isolation to the ways gender has been talked about in a range of international legal settings, or even domestic legal settings, would be reading too narrowly. For example, the deployment of passive gender roles for women fits with broader international human rights discourse that struggles to understand women as anything other than victims of human rights violations. The RRT went on to say that while it believed the woman would have to change her life, that she would be restricted in her movement and denied access to further opportunities of education, the Tribunal considered that this did not amount to persecution: it was not "systematic enough and severe enough to amount to persecution in the present circumstances" (RRT 1995, N95/09841, 20). The RRT then stated: "A man in a similar circumstance would find it intolerable to have his basic rights so curtailed in every area of his life based on the mere fact of his gender, and in Lebanon such would never happen to a man" (RRT 1995, N95/09841, 20).

The RRT is clearly stating that such practices against men could not be countenanced and, consequently, acknowledging clear differences in the ways women and men may consider themselves to be persecuted. The RRT is of the view that there are gendered abuses of human rights occurring in this case, but not persecution. Significant cultural and gendered baggage was evident in this narration in which refugee status was denied.

5.4   Case 4

The fourth case examined was made by a Lebanese woman on the basis of "particular social group", religion and nationality (RRT 1997, N97/14882), in which "particular social group" was based on her being a single unmarried woman in Lebanon who was pressured by her male relatives to get married. The RRT affirmed the decision.

The applicant was from a Maronite Christian family who lived in a village in southern Lebanon. During the 1980s Syrian forces took over their village and part of their family home. The applicant was raped by one of the soldiers who was at that time living in her home. After the woman told her mother about the rape, her mother yelled at the soldier. In retaliation he killed the mother and the woman's brother. The woman's family, after burying its dead, left town. Her father was insistent that she get married, but she was worried that he would find out she was not a virgin and try to avenge her attack. Her father tried to marry her to a man who had been in the militia. She then fled to Australia where her brother lived.

The RRT considered that the question in this case turned on whether she was raped for a reason included in the Convention, and found that she was raped:

> because as an individual she was home, alone, on a certain day when the Syrian officer—whose lustful look she had noticed and feared before—had also been at home and had had the opportunity to attack her. (RRT 1997, N97/14882, 6–7)

The woman was not attacked because of her membership of a particular social group or nationality but because of some uncanny coincidences—she was at home on a particular day when a Syrian officer was also at home. He was someone *she feared*. The RRT's narrative reduces the crime to a matter of opportunity—a theory well developed in criminology—such that if we simply reduce the opportunities to commit a particular crime then the crime will not be committed so often. Such an account places a heavy emphasis on individuals "protecting" themselves from being victimised. The word *lustful* serves to remove all political intent from the act of rape and instead positions the rape as a seemingly depoliticised and individualised sexual crime. Rape remains detached from the institutional, collective and occupational, cultural and gendered power of the armed forces. The above passage also positions the woman at odds with the ideal rape victim of international law (precarious legal subject at the best of times) on the grounds that: she knew her attacker (he occupied her house), she had previously been fearful (why hadn't she done anything?), she let herself be vulnerable ("home alone"), and the rape was in some way the result of a sexual relation already established ("lustful look she had noticed and feared before"). She does not conform to the ideal rape victim of international human rights who is raped along with many other women by faceless agents of the state never seen before or again. The rape becomes a matter between individuals, which distances it from the visibility of state-inflicted pain that the woman needs to establish.

Literal and interpretive denial was at work when the RRT went on to state:

> I do not accept that the fact that a few other girls in the village had been similarly attacked is evidence of there being a particular social group of raped Maronite women to which the applicant could have belonged. That the attacked girls were Maronites was because the village was Maronite. The girls would have been attacked not because they were Maronite but because they were individual objects of lust to soldiers and been vulnerable to molestation in particular circumstances. (RRT 1997, N97/14882, 7)

In "not accept[ing] that the fact that a few other girls in the village had been similarly attacked is evidence of there being a particular social group of raped Maronite women to which the applicant could have belonged" the RRT may have been advancing the legal precedent of the 1992 case heard in the Australian Federal Court, *Morato v Minister for Immigration, Local Government and Ethnic Affairs* (106 ALR 377), whereby the grounds for persecution cannot be defined by that persecution, but the narration can be read more deeply. The RRT member has thus become the bearer of reality in as much as the existence of a group of raped women becomes impossible *to* legally countenance and therefore is excluded from the discourse of gender-based persecution developed and eventually denied in the transcript. Perhaps the existence of a group of raped Maronite woman is impossible to countenance in relation to the precedent set in the Morato case, but to deny its existence apart from such a precedent is to diminish the existence of the woman making the claim as well as claims regarding the use of rape in conflict. There are now significant bodies of evidence regarding the use of rape in conflict (see, for example, Indra, 1999) upon which the RRT member could have drawn when denying the group's claim on Australian domestic refugee law, while still acknowledging the group's existence socially and politically within their community. As the passage reads on, rape becomes transposed to "molestation", and the women's ethnicity is not read as intersecting with gender to inform the relations of power that characterise life in an occupied village. Legal denial is extended when the RRT member states:

> I am unable to find that any rape would be for a reason of membership of any group of "single women in Lebanon", that is, for reasons of being one of those jointly condemned in the eyes of their persecutors, as opposed to being a random act of criminal behaviour. (RRT 1997, N97/14882, 7)

It is not only this rape, but all rapes that are disconnected from being a single, hence often vulnerable, woman. According to the RRT's commentary, the body that is "single woman" is disconnected from the use of rape in anything but a random fashion. Yet the random nature of rape established in this decision is then reflected upon in relation to collective levels of harassment in the Global South:

> Although harassment is probably no higher than in Latin America or southern Europe, and lower than in almost any other Arab country. (RRT 1997, N97/14882, 5)

The Tribunal's point here is clear: in countries such as Lebanon there is an expected (and therefore somehow acceptable) level of harassment. Reconciling the woman before the RRT to this harassment (again diminishing the incident in terms of the legal significance of sexual violence) becomes a slip of cultural relativism and paternalistic imperialism that allows the RRT to pronounce what may be expected when living a particular life in a particular place.

The RRT went on to consider that the pressure to marry is not an issue for the applicant given the "recent freedoms" she was able to demonstrate, and "[l]ogically, any pressure to marry would be because the applicant is single" (RRT 1997, N97/14882, 8). The matter was awaiting the imposed rationality of the RRT member to make sense of the pressure placed on the woman. It was then suggested that the woman had resisted marriage long enough and would be able to continue to do so:

> However, since she has grown to maturity without being married I find that she has been able to withstand that pressure successfully, earn an independent living and travel abroad independently.... (RRT 1997, N97/14882, 8)

The RRT then mused that alternatively she might persuade her brothers to talk to their father to change his mind. Fleeing to Australia was interpreted as "travelling abroad independently". The issue was thus concluded with the assertion that she had successfully "withstood pressure" to marry but now needed masculine assistance to change her father's mind.

5.5 Case 5

The fifth case examined was made by a woman from the Philippines on the grounds of "particular social group" (RRT 1993, N93/00656). The RRT set aside the decision. This is an important decision as "particular social group" was developed in depth in this case, and the decision has since been referred to in a number of other RRT and Federal Court decisions. A decision such as the one in this case distinguishes the complex ideological work undertaken by different Tribunal members (and hence the operation and review of refugee status determination).

The woman had experienced domestic violence over a period of 27 years in a forced marriage in which her movements were restricted, and her husband had threatened to kill her on a number of occasions, including putting a gun to her head. She argued that she was a member of the "particular social group" of women who had experienced domestic violence. The RRT rejected this on the basis that the enunciated grounds could not be defined by the persecution experienced (Hathaway, 1991; Shacknove, 1985; Greatbatch, 1989; Arboleda & Hoy, 1993). The RRT, nonetheless, went on to define "particular social group" as:

> The shared social characteristics common to all women relate to gender and either emanate from, or are generally perceived to emanate from, gender. They include the ability to give birth, the role of principal child-rearers, nurturers, keepers of the family home, supportive partners in a relationship. And, as in the present case, it is commonly expected throughout most societies that it is characteristic of women to remain loyal to their husbands, to keep marriages together, regardless of their treatment within marriage. It is the RRT's view therefore that women form a cognisable group in accordance with the principles espoused in Morato. (RRT 1993, N93/00656, 20)

The RRT continued by asserting that the existence of separate services for women in different societies provides an example of how women are perceived as being a separate social group:

> That Australian society regards women as a particular social group warranting particular attention, is evidenced by the establishment of various Commonwealth bodies such as the Office of the Status of Women…that women share a common social status is evident from the fact that women generally earn less than men and that few women hold positions of power in both government and non-government institutions…. Another element bonding all women, regardless of culture or class, is that of the fear of being subjected to male violence. (RRT 1993, N93/00656, 21)

Significantly, this decision draws on other human rights conventions and UNHCR guidelines:

> Whilst it is the case that this application has to be determined in accordance with the Refugee Convention and Protocol, nonetheless the International Covenants on Human Rights and UNHCR Guidelines are properly given significance. (RRT 1993, N93/00656, 15)

The suggestion that separate services evidence women as a particular social group was later rejected by the RRT in a case in which the UNHCR Guidelines were also rejected (RRT 1998, N98/22513).

This case represents an important point of departure in the examination of the narration of gender and "particular social group". The decision legally acknowledges acts of gender-based persecution and hence clarifies the level of responsibility on the part of the RRT in responding to these acts. It is clear from this decision that individualising persecution to the extent of reducing it to a random or explainable criminal act does not have to be automatic. The decision locates international refugee law clearly within the ambit of the field of human rights law and supports issues around gender and "particular social group" by drawing on wider understandings of gender established in human rights law.

The cited "shared social characteristics" common to all women are also problematic. They invoke gendered stereotypes that exclude many women who do not undertake such social functions or who reject such roles. So even when a positive decision attempts to open up new spaces for the discussion of gender and "particular social group", the narration may still ignore the multiple meanings gender may have for different women in different places at different times.

Attempting to squeeze gender into the category "particular social group" remains a flawed project. It is flawed because underpinning the narration of gender and "particular social group" exists a highly essentialising discourse. For example, it is much more difficult, but by no means impossible, to essentialise gender within grounds of race or political opinion, and when Tribunal members do consider women's claims within these grounds, rather than "particular social group", such essentialising gender narratives fade. In particular, we must investigate whether the use of political opinion as the home for claims of gender-based persecution has the potential to politicise gender.

In the period 2003–2009 nine cases based on the fear of FGM and particular social group were appealed to the Australian RRT. Seven cases were brought by women, and two cases by men fearing harm to their wife, sister or daughter. All involved fear of FGM being committed for the first time. Both appeals made by males along with two of the appeals made by women were rejected. The remaining five cases were ordered to be reconsidered by the RRT following intervention either by the Minister for Immigration or the superior courts. All nine cases were brought in 2009.

6   The Judicial Operation of the Gate

Pressure has increased on the Obama administration to develop and release formal policy guidelines on the administration of asylum claims based on gender-based persecution following a recent high-profile and protracted case in the United States involving domestic violence. This pressure has become intertwined with ongoing campaigns to remove the one-year bar on asylum applications that are lodged more than 12 months after the applicant's arrival in the United States.

Rody Alvarado fled extreme battering at the hands of her husband, a former member of the military, in Guatemala. Her "iconic" case, initiated in 1995 and determined in 2009, can be regarded as a litmus test for the refugee policies of the three US administrations that considered, and reconsidered, her case. Following an adverse ruling by an immigration judge in 1996, the then Attorney-General Janet Reno overturned the decision, but did not grant her asylum. Instead, she issued regulations recognising gender-based persecution as a possible basis for asylum. However, these guidelines were never released. Following disputes between government departments that share responsibility for refugee matters—namely, Homeland

Security and Justice—the Bush administration left office having not made a final determination on the *Alvarado* case. In September 2008, the then Attorney-General Michael Mukasey sent the case back to the immigration appeals court, encouraging the court to issue a precedent-setting ruling. In October 2009, the Department of Homeland Security filed documents before the immigration courts that detailed that Ms Alvarado was eligible for asylum as a grant of discretion. Thus, this decision does not create a precedent for similar cases that might follow.

The *Alvarado* case came following a period of regression in the campaign to legally recognise women's asylum claims on the basis of gender-based violence. In 1996 the *Kasinga* case was internationally acclaimed when it determined that FGM establishes that a woman belongs to a particular social group, but not that FGM was a specific ground for asylum. Fauziya Kassindja fled Togo fearing FGC and forced marriage when she was 17 years old. She was denied asylum because she was considered not to be a credible witness and that FGC did not constitute grounds for an asylum claim. On appeal, the BIA significantly advanced jurisprudence of asylum and gender-based persecution.

This ground-breaking case established that FGC is a form of persecution that has permanent and ongoing effects. The *Kasinga* case has been drawn upon by jurisdictions in Australia, New Zealand, Canada and the United Kingdom. FGC has now been advanced as grounds for asylum in a number of jurisdictions since the 1980s, all based on arguments that the practice amounts to gender-based persecution.[3] International organisations including the UN have investigated the practice since the 1950s when the Commission of the Status of Women, the Economic and Social Council (ECOSOC) and the General Assembly all adopted resolutions encouraging its abolition, asserting that the practice violates human rights (Charlesworth & Chinkin, 2000). However, responses to how this should or could be achieved were diverse and often controversial, with bodies such as the World Health Organization (WHO) asserting that because these were ritual and cultural practices they were beyond its remit. By the early 1980s the matter was again on the international agenda, specifically as a health issue, which in turn raised a series of arguments relating to whether it could be practised in a medically acceptable way that minimised the risks to women. As Charlesworth and Chinkin's account of the international response shows, by the early 1990s the General Assembly, through the *Declaration on the Elimination of Violence against Women*, had defined the practice as harmful to women.[4]

---

[3] For example, *Yake v Secretary of State for the Home Department,* 19 January 2000, unreported; *P and M v Secretary of State for the Home Department* [2004] EWCA Civ 1640 [2005] Imm AR 84), *Abankwah v Immigration and Naturalization Service* 185 F 3d 18 (2d Cir 1999), *Mohammed v Gonzales 400* F 3d 785 (9th Cir 2005), Australia *(RRT N97119046,* 16 October 1997), and Canada *(Re B(PV)* [1994] CRDD No 12, 10 May 1994).

[4] Charlesworth and Chinkin provide a useful overview of the debate between feminists of the Global South and Global North.

7 Refugee Determination and Female Genital Cutting: Gate Open, Gate Shut, Gate Open, Gate Shut

While the *Kasinga* case has provided an important legal precedent it has not been encapsulated in statute or regulation, meaning the rules for making such a determination are open to reinterpretation and challenge. In 2007, two decisions undermined the advances in the legal recognition of women's claims for asylum in the United States. For the purposes of this chapter the most notable is the *Matter of A-T-*, in which the BIA concluded that FGC is a one-time harm and therefore women who have already been subjected to FGC have no reason to fear being cut again and hence are not eligible for refugee protection. It is important to recognise that the *Matter of A-T-* also seriously undermined the influence of the *Kasinga* case by concluding that a father is not eligible for withholding of removal on the grounds of a fear for his daughter's safety from FGC in his home country (see Frydman & Seelinger, 2008 for a detailed discussion).

Since the *Kasinga* case, US courts and tribunals have been willing to accept arguments that a woman who has not yet been cut may have a well-founded fear of future persecution because of the likelihood of being subjected to the practice and/or other forms of serious harm she may experience as part of communal punishment or ostracism for having resisted the practice (see, for example, *Mohammed v Gonzales*). Following *In re Y-T-L*, it was also accepted that women who have already been subjected to FGC could successfully mount a claim for asylum based on a fear of ongoing harm and persecution, which may include being recut following childbirth or prior to marriage as well as the ongoing physical and psychological consequences of such harm. The lynchpin of such cases is that for women who had already been cut their ongoing well-founded fear need not be the same as that experienced in relation to the original persecution—in short, that a woman would not need to establish that she would experience precisely the same form of harm if she returned to her country of origin.

It is important to note that while the *Kasinga* case established a significant legal precedent, applicants have still been required to adequately demonstrate the likelihood of being subjected to FGC and other serious harm upon their return home, and are still confronted by doubts as to their credibility as a witness. It is also notable that experienced attorneys who have represented women in FGC cases have outlined that to mount a successful claim (see, for example, Frydman & Seelinger, 2008) the key legal elements need to be accompanied by astute legal argument that contextualises the claims in an informed account of broader female subjugation and risk, the difficulties of fleeing the situation and detailed understandings of the physical and psychological impact.

In the 1996 UK case of *Fornah*, the applicant was from Sierra Leone. As outlined earlier, at the age of 15 she arrived in the United Kingdom and claimed asylum on the basis that she would be subjected to FGC if she were to return to Sierra Leone.

The judgement in *Fornah* drew heavily on guidance from the European Parliament (European Parliament Resolution A5-0285/2001), who resolved in 2001 that

European institutions and member states should recognise the right to asylum of women and girls at risk of being subjected to FGM, as well as drawing on gender guidelines issued by national authorities in Canada, Australia and more recently in the United Kingdom. It also interpreted the recently released EU Qualification Directive, which was more ambiguous in defining "particular social group", and in plain terms suggested a cumulative reading of the social perception and protected characteristics approaches. The social perception test, formulated in the Australian case of *A v Minister for Immigration and Ethnic Affairs*, required that PSG be objectively established by reference to how a group is perceived by the society in which it exists. It has been criticised because in attempting to establish an "objective" test it relies almost exclusively on subjective assessment of how societies perceive groups. The protected characteristics approach, which is informed by anti-discrimination principles, was formulated in the case of *Re Acosta* and the Canadian decision in the 1997 case of *Ward*. The judgement in *Fornah* argued for an either/or approach to social perception or protected characteristics rather than a cumulative assessment, as suggested by a plain reading of the document (Chaudhry, 2007). The judgements in *Fornah* also distinguished themselves from the Court of Appeal decision which they reversed, by drawing heavily on the international literature on the discriminatory treatment and human rights of women and girls in concluding that FGM is an extreme expression of discrimination and of women's subservient position in society.

The unanimous decision to grant asylum to Fornah expressed a degree of contempt of earlier judgements adopted unduly restrictive readings of the Refugee Convention to refuse applications based on gender-based persecution, as well as some exasperation that such cases required protracted legal argument and process. Historically, the majority of judicial decisions on "particular social group" have opted for a narrow interpretation, and in fact exclusionary approaches to "particular social group" have been *de rigueur* in most jurisdictions, legal platitudes concerning the "regrettable" nature and outcomes of gendered discrimination and persecution have predominated over the difficult legal work necessary to include gender-based violence within the meaning of the Convention. Commentators have noted that the decision in *Fornah* made the prior decision of the Court of Appeal to deny the application appear to be making "all the right noises about how awful FGM is" before taking "sanctuary in a mean and narrow interpretation of the law". In the House of Lords Baroness Hale of Richmond said:

> The answer in each case is so blindingly obvious that it must be a mystery to some why either of them had to reach this House. (Baroness Hale in Secretary of State for the Home Department v. K (Fe); Fornah (Fe) v. Secretary of State for the Home Department [2006] 83)

The Court of Appeal had found in the case of *Fornah* that because not all women in Sierra Leonean society opposed the practice, and once a woman was subjected to FGM she no longer faced further threat of persecution and because FGC was practised by many women, she did not meet the criteria for "particular social group" and hence refugee protection. The Court of Appeal concluded: "…however harshly we may stigmatise the practice as persecution for the purpose of article 3 it is not, in the circumstances in which it is practiced in Sierra Leone, discriminatory in such a way as to set those who undergo it apart from society" (at 44 in the judgement). This conclusion, condemned by the House of Lords decision, has also attracted scathing criticism: "It is nothing less than deplorable that the arguments that not all women in society opposed FGM and some women collaborated in the practice.... This conclusion was reached in spite of compelling evidence clearly establishing FGM as a serious human rights violation" (Chaudhry, 2007, p. 7).

The case of *Fornah* is notable for Hale's explicit recognition of difference and that the Refugee Convention must provide protection not only to men. Baroness Hale's overt recognition of gender-related and gender-specific persecution "haunts the unanimous ruling" (Rackley, 2008, p. 38). She asserted that the world may have "woken up to the fact that women as a sex may be persecuted in ways which are different from the ways in which men are persecuted" (Baroness Hale, *Fornah* [2006] 86).

Her judgement has been widely welcomed for its explicit destabilisation of dominant forms of knowledge that undergird judicial understanding of gender generally, and gender-based persecution specifically. Rackley has argued that the judgement of Baroness Hale, while consistent with those of the other judges with whom she was in furious agreement, offered something different by taking account of difference. However, it is not only the substance of her judgement that is significant, but also its use of common-sense logic in countering the tangle of legal arguments surrounding what may precisely be seen as constituting a "particular social group". For example, Hale reminds us:

> ...it cannot make any difference that [FGM] is practised by women upon women and girls. Those who have already been persecuted are often expected to perpetuate the persecution of others, as any reader of *Tom Brown's Schooldays* knows. (p. 110)

Rackley (2008) points out that in her shoot-from-the-hip style the Baroness is engaging in a discursive narrative as opposed to the restrained legal reasoning of her male counterparts. However, what is plain from examining a series of illustrative examples from cases from Australia, the United Kingdom and the United States is that even within restrained legal reasoning—which has so often resulted in denial of claims for asylum grounded on gender-based persecution—a discursive narrative is taking place, albeit often more subtle and cloaked in the "restrictions" that the Refugee Convention requires of decision-makers. Therefore, the detailed narrative that Hale develops in fact matches in substance, and arguably outflanks in style, more traditional approaches to accounting for gender. For example, in the case of *Fornah* Justices Hope and Rodger sought to explicitly differentiate the claims of women who may be at risk of being subjected to the practice for the first time from those of women who have already been cut and who claim asylum for reasons of ongoing persecution. They did so by expressing their preference for defining "particular social group" narrowly and would be as exclusive as possible in any given circumstances. Lord Hope of Craighead said:

> So one can say, with greater precision, that the particular social group is composed of uninitiated indigenous females in Sierra Leone. I do not think that there can be any objection to defining the group in these terms. It has the advantage of excluding from the group those who have already been initiated. They can never be said under any circumstances to

be still at risk. It has the advantage too of excluding those who carry out the mutilation, all of whom have already been initiated. It excludes also those females who, although living in Sierra Leone, are not at risk because they are not members of any tribe or ethnic group which is indigenous to that country. These advantages suggest that in this case precision to that extent is desirable. But I see no need to go any further than that. (Lord Hope of Craighead, at 56)

And Lord Rodger of Earlsferry concurred:

So, unusually, this is a form of persecution which the persecutor will wish to carry out only once, however long the victim lives. (at 71)

In contrast, Baroness Hale dissented when she took a far more robust (Edwards, 2007) stance that gender is itself enough to constitute a particular social group for the purposes of the Convention definition. Her nuanced understanding of gender, and the common-sense application should the position of the sexes be reversed, has communicatory flair:

The stumbling block seems to have been the fact that FGM is a once and for all event. Once done, it can neither be undone nor repeated. Thus, it was argued, if many members of the group are no longer at risk, because they have already suffered, it can no longer constitute a group for this purpose. But if the group has to be defined only to include those at risk, it then looks as if the group is defined solely by the risk of persecution and nothing more. This is a peculiarly cruel version of Catch 22: if not all the group are at risk, then the persecution cannot be caused by their membership of the group; if the group is reduced to those who are at risk, it is then defined by the persecution alone. But the reasoning is fallacious at a number of levels. It is the persecution, not the fear, which has to be "by reason of" membership of the group. Even if the group is reduced to those who are currently intact, its members share many characteristics which are independent of the persecution—their gender, their nationality, their ethnicity. It is those characteristics which lead to the persecution, not the persecution itself which leads to those characteristics. But there is no need to reduce the group to those at risk. It is well settled that not all members of the group need be at risk. There is nothing in the Convention to say that all members have to be susceptible. It should not matter why they are not at risk. If the authorities of a particular State had a policy of mutilating all male members of a particular tribe or sect by cutting off their right hands, we would still say that the intact members of the tribe or sect faced persecution because of their membership of the tribe or sect rather than because of their intactness. (Hale at 112–113)

The interpretation and development of PSG as grounds for asylum has been described as erratic and capricious (Musalo, 2008), incremental and unprincipled (Chaudhry, 2007). For the purposes of understanding the extent to which the Refugee Convention offers a workable gate for women who cross borders seeking asylum, it is apparent that when the courts have been faced with the option of broadening their interpretation of the Convention to offer predictable application of protection from gender-based persecution—and enacting the humanitarian objectives of the Convention, they have opted instead to protect the interests of the states affording protection (see Chaudhry, 2007). As Chaudhry (2007) has argued, "The need to establish tighter border controls is prioritised far more highly than giving effect to the humanitarian goals of the Refugee Convention. I therefore anticipate that, despite the resounding strength of their Lordships' judgements, the principles established in *Fornah* will have limited impact on Convention jurisprudence" (Chaudhry, 2007, p. 10). Indeed, a series of recent decisions in the United Kingdom from the Asylum and Immigration Tribunal and elsewhere have indicated that this is likely to be the case, and Chaudhry further notes that without clearer European directives PSG will remain unstable despite the strength of specific rulings such as that in *Fornah*.

8   The Matter of A-T-

In relation to the *Matter of A-T-,* Musalo (2008) offers a theory about why the board treated forced sterilisation differently from genital cutting. Sterilisation affects procreation and motherhood, which are valued by men. Genital cutting, by contrast, affects "only" women's sexual pleasure and autonomy.

The 2007 US *Matter of A-T-* involved a claim for asylum by a woman from Mali who as a child had been subjected to FGC. After arriving in the United States on a student visa in 2000 she attended college and studied nursing. The applicant was subsequently contacted by her father, who demanded that she return to Mali and marry her first cousin. Her father threatened her with a range of punitive consequences should she not comply with his wishes. Her claim for asylum made in 2004 was based on her experience of being subjected to FGC, its ongoing consequences and the threat of forced marriage. Her initial application was considered ineligible because it was not made within 12 months of her being in the United States.

In considering the application made in the *Matter of A-T-* the BIA found that if a woman had already been subjected to FGC then the fear of persecution would have ceased because she had already suffered the harm she feared. On this account, FGC may amount to persecution requiring protection, but it also becomes the basis for denying that protection—the persecution has already happened and therefore will not happen again. In essence, the Board here rejected that there could be any ongoing persecutory impacts from FGC and that the persecution itself amounted to changed conditions (even though governing regulations were specifically concerned with *country* conditions not *general* conditions, or general conditions *in addition* to country conditions). As Frydman and Seelinger (2008) note, the circularity of this reasoning had already been recognised as producing an "anomalous" result in previous BIA decisions in cases of forced sterilisation and abortion, decisions that were based on the view that if one had already been sterilised or forced to abort then there could be no fear of this occurring again:

> It is illogical to find that a political dissident whose tongue was cut out could be found to have no future fear of harm on account of her political opinion merely because she cannot again lose her tongue. Or that a man whose house is burned down on account of his tribal identity fears no future danger since that house has already been destroyed. (Frydman & Seelinger, 2008, p. 1080)

In the *Matter of A-T-* the Board differentiated the case from *Kasinga* by drawing on the case of *Oforji v Ashcroft*[5]: "In Kasinga, however, the applicant had not yet

---

[5] 354 F.3d 609, 615 (7th Cir: 2003).

undergone FGM and was facing an imminent threat of being subjected to the procedure if returned to her country of origin. The respondent in this case had already undergone FGM." Consequently, even assuming arguendo that she is a member of a particular social group who has suffered past persecution, "there is no chance that she would be personally [persecuted] again by the procedure" (at 299).

The *Oforji* case is a controversial point of reference because the application for asylum was based on a derivative claim that the applicant's daughters (who had US citizenship) would be subjected to FGM if they returned to Nigeria with her. The applicant had experienced FGM and was seeking to remain in the United States. The Court made a ruling in which it focused on the importance of not opening the floodgates to applicants with children who come to the United States and then seek asylum as a means of securing their own legal status in the United States. By contrast, the *Matter of A-T-* rejected the decision of *Mohammed v Gonzales* in 2005 that found that FGM constitutes a continuing harm for purposes of asylum in line with the prior decision in *Kasinga*. The *Matter of A-T-* continues:

> Any presumption of future FGM persecution is thus rebutted by the fundamental change in the respondent's situation arising from the reprehensible, but one time, infliction of FGM upon her. (at 299)

The BIA had relied upon the introduction of concerns regarding sterilisation and abortion in the *Immigration and Nationality Act*, which sought to increase the efficiency of the courts in recognising such practices as forms of persecution. In the *Matter of A-T-* the Board inferred that if Congress had wanted FGC to occupy a similarly privileged place they would have specified it in the legislation. Drawing on the *Matter of Y-T-L-* in which involuntary sterilisation and abortion represented an exception to the principle of ongoing persecution, the Board claimed:

> ...because persons who suffered such harm have been singled out by Congress as having a basis of asylum in the refugee definition of section 101(a)(42) of the Act on the strength of the past harm alone. While FGM is similar to forced sterilization in the same sense that it is a harm that is normally performed only once but has ongoing physical and emotional effects, Congress has not seen fit to recognize FGM (or any other specific kind of persecution) in a similar fashion with special statutory provisions. Hence, we deem it consistent with the statutory and regulatory scheme to view FGM in the same category as most other past injuries that rise to the level of persecution, including those that involve some lasting disability such as the loss of a limb. (p. 300)

FGC was compared in the judgement to "The loss of a limb [which] also gives rise to enduring harm to the victim, but such forms of past persecution are routinely assessed under the past persecution standards specified in the asylum and withholding of removal regulations" (p. 301).

In short, the Board determined in the *Matter of A-T-* that FGC is not special like sterilisation and abortion because it lacks the legitimation of statute. Without such regulatory shelter the Board found that the anomalous rationale—that the persecution could be the reason for not granting protection—could not be avoided in cases of FGC unlike cases of sterilisation and abortion:

> ...in sharp contrast, there is no separate statutory ground of persecution predicated on an alien's being subjected to FGM. Consequently, there is no basis for following an approach

outside the regulatory formula for assessing persecution claims founded on past persecution alone. (p. 300)

Frydman and Seelinger (2008) have argued that such reasoning is disingenuous because the legislative amendments in relation to sterilisation and forced abortion were not introduced to privilege these two forms of persecution, but rather came as a result of the inability of Chinese applicants to demonstrate the nexus between persecution and protected ground. In short, the system had come to rely on understanding forced sterilisations and abortions in China as a generalised policy, and not one that singled out individuals for persecution. The legislation in question was introduced to remove unduly restrictive court readings of the Refugee Convention. This was in contrast to legislation introduced in Australia following progressive gender rulings in asylum claims, which sought to further restrict application of the Convention to gender-based claims. Frydman and Seelinger (2008) further argued that the *Matter of A-T-* "constitutes an unexplained and troubling departure from the agency's prior determinations" (p. 1083), which has since had significant deleterious impacts on applications concerning FGC. Moreover, attorneys representing women in claims for asylum based on either future or past FGC deemed ineligible because of the one-year bar have been advised that such claims be asserted simultaneously with claims of corollary harms faced by women fleeing FGC, including but not limited to domestic violence, rape, forced marriage and other forms of sexual violence.

In the United States the division of responsibility regarding immigration between the Departments of Homeland Security and Justice has militated against the emergence of a consensus position on regulating for the recognition of gender-based persecution.

Decision-makers have opted for either restrictive or more flexible readings of the Convention in order to either incorporate or reject women's experiences of persecution. Even with non-binding direction from UNHCR, the EU, and guidelines from relevant departments, what the illustrative cases demonstrate is that individually and collectively the interpretation results in erratic and capricious decision-making.

9   A Case for Gender Guidelines

The release of the UNHCR *Guidelines on International Protection: Gender-Related Persecution* was well received internationally. However, the Guidelines rely on a bifurcated system of recognising gender persecution: on the one hand, sophisticated court-based decisions; and, on the other, under-scrutinised primary decisions that act more as routine gatekeepers for women's asylum claims.

Decision-makers at the primary or first stage merits review level rarely have the time to engage with the many contradictions such Guidelines raise in carrying out the daily business of determining refugee status. A commitment to protecting women from gender-based persecution that accurately aligns with the Convention definition requires effective procedural realisation at the initial interview stage if it is to protect women. Thus, we must question how the UNHCR Guidelines can be implemented at this initial decision-making state. Furthermore, this question is coupled with another: what role do these Guidelines play in preventing governments from legislating away from the intent of the Convention, or preventing policy and practice from recognising gender-based persecution as outlined within the current Convention? It is clear that we must seize the intent and spirit of recognising gender-based persecution as reflected by the development of these Guidelines, and acknowledge and address their assumptions and omissions, and their potential for marginalisation, if we are to reach a position where we can establish effective protection of women from gender-based persecution under the Refugee Convention.

The punitive trend in refugee protection within developed nations has been marked by watershed moments in relation to issues raised by, or in direct response to, cases of gender-based persecution. Gender-based persecution has often acted as the moment to usher in more restrictive refugee protection policies for all those seeking asylum in the developed world. Therefore, the concern here is how we can consider these Guidelines as a bugger to the many issues raised by gender-based persecution for refugee determination procedures in general, but also whether these Guidelines take adequate account of how the recognition of persecution is often used by developed nations to signal that the system is out of control, that refugee protection is in need of containment and that the international refugee regime needs to be reformed.

The UNHCR Guidelines talk about a "gender-sensitive interpretation" of the Convention. The term "sensitive" suggests a need for compassion, for kindness. Cases of gender-based persecution require complex and detailed knowledge of how human rights apply to the multifaceted and diverse lives of women in a non-discriminatory way. While sensitivity is to be commended, perhaps even encouraged, women are not being turned away at borders or having their cases rejected by primary decision-makers because the latter are insensitive. They are turned away in particular because the primary decisions made have been inaccurate and discriminatory, and decision-makers have located themselves, their government and the women applicants at a great distance from human rights.

The Guidelines make clear that not all of the women of the world will be able to claim protection under the Convention. In this moment of rejection, the spectre of hordes of women is still raised, similar to the well-worn "threat" of "hordes of Asians" or "entire Middle Eastern villages" seeking to claim asylum. I am unaware of any statements on race or nationality or religion that similarly reassure decision-makers, governments and the public with the comment that indeed not all people of religion or who have a certain nationality are automatically entitled to protection under the Convention. The Guidelines read:

> Adopting a gender sensitive interpretation of the 1951 Convention does not mean that all women are automatically entitled to refugee status. The refugee claimant must establish that he or she has a well founded fear of being persecuted for reasons of race, religion, nationality, membership of a particular social group or political opinion. (UNHCR Guidelines, 2002)

Gender is not something to strap down or contain. Seriously redressing gender-based persecution is about living up to the principles of non-discrimination and should not be intimidated by the spectre of unproven numbers (Mathew, 2000).

In considering the Background Paper commissioned by the UNHCR Global Consultations on International Protection on Gender Related Persecution by Haines I found little with which to take issue and much to reinforce. Suffice to say that if decision-makers at all levels took a similarly informed, complex and rights-based approach, women seeking asylum would be more able to predict the outcome of their applications. The UNHCR Guidelines on Gender Persecution released in May 2002 may in part capture the depth of issues outlined in the Background Paper. However, I have a number of reservations about the Guidelines most specifically in relation to what I consider to be the three most serious omissions. The Guidelines fail to: provide clear and compelling statements that locate refugee law within international human rights law; significantly address cultural relativism in decision-making; or tackle the site at which the issue of gender persecution sustains heavy attack—women's credibility. These three areas are consistently at the core of cases of gender persecution, and considering the discussion of the first two in the Background Paper, they are notable by their absence in the Guidelines. These three omissions signal that the Guidelines do not seriously contribute to advancing critical understanding and practice in refugee determination, and thereby sit comfortably within frameworks that consider protection to be an act of gratuitous humanity and refuse to challenge the assumptions and practices of primary decision-makers at the borders of the Global North.

9.1 Absence of a Human Rights Framework

The Guidelines struggle to locate gender persecution and the Refugee Convention within the broader field of human rights law. The Guidelines use the term "human rights" in five places with no articulation of a human rights framework for gender persecution claims specifically or refugee law generally (with the exception of a footnote). Failing to locate gender persecution and refugee law within international human rights law goes against the agenda of burgeoning scholarly literature on gender persecution and refugee law (see, for example, Crawley, 2001). Second, the Guidelines need to locate gender persecution within international human rights if they are to offer any resistance to the legislative "wiping away" of gains made in these areas.

We know that claims for gender-based persecution, and decisions that have upheld those claims, have consistently relied on integrating gender persecution and the Convention with other international treaties (Kelly, 2002). Moreover, feminist scholars working to raise understanding of gender persecution have argued for what Mathew (2000) has called a synergy between the Refugee Convention and general human rights law. The Refugee Convention as a stand-alone document is rarely enough to realise women's claims for refugee status. The Guidelines on gender persecution need to compel decision-makers to read the Convention within the context of a body of human rights law and acknowledge refugee law as an application of human rights norms (Anker, 2002). This will help dislodge readings of refugee law that are immovably embedded in domestic immigration law and engage a dialogue between refugee law and human rights law that can sustain what Anker has called a rich body of "trans-national international law".

Through the rapidly evolving field of women's human rights, a consideration of gender persecution has helped drive refugee law and human rights law together, entailing benefits not only for cases of gender persecution. It is also from international human rights that we strongly argue for locating gender perspectives within a sophisticated reading of the current Convention and argue against an additional ground of gender. The normative potential of the Guidelines has been avoided by the absence of clear and detailed statements on the relationship between refugee law and human rights law. Keeping gender persecution precariously poised, conditional and delicate means that both gender and asylum are left to move in parallel to, but certainly apart from, human rights. Moreover, this situation presents receiving states in the Global North with another moment of refugee guidance that is unrestrained by international human rights.

It has been acknowledged that the legal wrangling over whether gender-based persecution is being adequately covered within the existing refugee definition has been "dominated by Western developed countries seeking to demark the limits of refugee protection" (Kelly, 2002, p. 560). The tension between immigration control and the application of refugee law in accordance with standards of international human rights has been played out in some cases in the shadow that is the postured millions of refugee women now seeking protection. This is despite the fact that any right to Convention protection has never meant that protection has been readily or predictably accorded to women. In response to decision-makers according women protection, governments have sought to legislate away the interconnectedness of gender persecution, refugee protection and international human rights.

The case of *Khawar* (*MIMA v Khawar*, HCA 11 April 2002), and the legislative response of the Australian Parliament to this case, is an example of how embracing the synergy among gender persecution, refugee law and international human rights law has been considered by developed nations as going beyond the "proper interpretation" of the Convention. In working to narrow the application of refugee protection the Immigration Minister used the case of *Khawar* as evidence that the Australian courts and tribunals had been interpreting the Refugee Convention too broadly and in a way that went beyond its intended application. The Migration Amendment Bill (no. 6) 2001 was therefore introduced to "restore the application of the Convention...in Australia to its proper interpretation" (Ruddock, 2002, p. 1). The legislation introduced a much more narrow and rigid interpretation of the Convention that is at odds with the kind of sophisticated and complex reasoning given in the *Khawar* decision, and now has a disproportionate impact on women applicants (Hunter, 2002, p. 107). Most of all, the legislative response to the *Khawar* case can be seen to constitute a moment to restrict the application of human rights norms and the Refugee Convention to cases of gender-based persecution, extending restrictive determination to all asylum applications. Locating gender-based persecution within international human rights law, and hence recognising the changing nature of the traditional subjects of international law, as the *Khawar* decision did, came to represent the troublesome nature of the judiciary and the repugnance of human rights for the realisation of domestic refugee policy and border control.

9.2   Ignoring the Role of Cultural Relativism

The Guidelines have missed an opportunity to resuscitate refugee determination from the paralysis that is cultural relativism. Whereas some commentators have noted that the challenge of cultural relativism stems from an unresolved theoretical stand-off (Anker, 2002), I suggest that these challenges are far more ordinary and everyday. Reaching for simplistic cultural explanations of gender persecution devoid of any developed understanding of violence against women does see some women gain asylum. However, both sexist and cultural stereotypes rely on essentialist understandings of gender and the Global South.

There is now a growing body of research that points to how decision-makers depend on linking gender-based persecution to practices of "non-western foreign cultures" (Sinha, 2001). In short, without the clear "foreignness" of a cultural practice, gender persecution has often been dismissed or overlooked by decision-makers. The search by decision-makers for what Sinha has called "cultural culpability" in cases of gender persecution has marked key US cases such as *Kasinga*. Such accusations of cultural culpability are rooted in stereotypes about the helpless Third World woman, the wickedness of the Third World man and the backwardness of state protection. This produces refugee discourse that notably posits the cultural, political and legal superiority of Western life (Crawley, 2001). Some commentators have observed, for example, that writings on refugee law leave the impression that social mores only exist in Third World countries generally and Muslim countries specifically (Spijkerboer, 1994). Although culture is mentioned in the Guidelines, they do not make an adequately strong statement regarding the prevalence of misplaced cultural relativism in refugee determinations. As other parts of this chapter demonstrate, using such frames of reference means that the dehumanising structures from which women may have fled are reproduced in ways that Crawley argues infer that these women are alien to both their own culture and the culture of the receiving country. The refugee determination system has thus coerced particular performances of gender persecution whereby women's experiences are forced to fit within one of a few options readily consumable by the determination system. The Guidelines do not seriously address how cultural essentialism has been the easiest way for decision-makers to redress gender persecution and the consequences this has for the system, regardless of whether an individual woman gains asylum.

9.3   Credibility Issues

The Guidelines also do not directly address the issue of an applicant's credibility. This in some ways reflects the absence of a discussion of credibility issues in the Background Paper. When decision-makers have failed to grapple with the complexity that a rights-based approach requires, they have often returned to the issue of a woman's credibility. Credibility is of course at the heart of refugee determination, particularly in cases of gender persecution where detailed and trustworthy independent accounts of the role and position of women in the country of origin are lacking. The issue of credibility is often raised in relation to whether the woman failed to engage state protection or whether her account of the failure of state protection is adequate. There is a long and disturbing history of women around the world being rendered child-like, manipulative or simply unbelievable in their demeanour by courts. The Guidelines, I believe, need to offer decision-makers greater guidance as to what is a serious credibility issue and what is not. A clear articulation of credibility issues would directly tackle the struggle over the standard of proof in asylum applications relating to gender persecution.

There is considerable evidence in psychological research that, in recounting traumatic experiences, many people who try to accurately describe experiences that occurred over a period of weeks, months or even years often amend their memories, and introduce new elements and delete others, over the course of a series of interviews. Research indicates that this was not an attempt to sustain a lie, but rather to ensure that the story they tell is as accurate as possible. However, too often such amendment is viewed as evidence of a lack of credibility. This situation is compounded for women recounting stories of rape and sexual violence, as they may be reluctant, for a range of reasons, to reveal the details of such experiences as part of their narrative in initial interviews.

Crawley (2001) has noted that many women face additional problems in demonstrating that their claims are credible. The most significant issue regarding credibility has been the timing of women's claims of gender persecution. Often women are considered to lack credibility because they only disclose their experiences in the second interview or after their case has gone to appeal. The non-disclosure of sexual violence—though the reasons for which are well understood by many decision-makers—has seen many women's claims disregarded primarily because of their timing.

Doubts of women's credibility also exacerbate the stress and trauma they experience during initial interviewing, often at the border. In Australia, these interviews are conducted in the context of some form of detention, by those who have been flown thousands of kilometres to conduct the interviews and who are encouraged to process the maximum number of claims each day. The procedural recommendations of the Guidelines do not adequately take account of the environment in which the credibility of applicants is questioned or of the particular consequences this has for applicants making gender-based persecution claims.

The depiction of gender-based persecution has necessarily been problematic. Fitting gender-based persecution into the Refugee Convention definition, as the cases

outlined above demonstrate, has been very difficult, and often relies on essentialising gender, race and ethnicity. Those cases that have been successful have needed to
employ homogenising discourses of the Refugee Convention, and its interpretation
has been an untrustworthy form of human rights protection for women who have
experienced gender-based persecution—sometimes providing protection but only
where there has been a "cultural hook" (Sinha, 2001). Whereas some have argued
that such essentialising strategies reflect on the credibility of the applicant or the
unsophisticated strategy of the legal representative, it is, as this chapter has argued,
much more about what decision-makers are receptive to hearing in the context of
a history of unduly restrictive judicial interpretations of the Refugee Convention.

The difficulties of obtaining refugee status for women who have fled gender-
based persecution have arguably contributed to the increased development of forms
of complementary protection: ways of allowing women to stay in a country even
when their application for asylum has failed.

10   Recourse to Complementary Protection

Complementary protection is not consistently defined in international law. However, it is generally agreed that it refers to a form of protection that is based on a
need that falls outside the 1951 Refugee Convention. It has often included reference
to one or more human rights treaties or other humanitarian principles (McAdam,
2005). Such protection may have similar or different benefits to refugee status, and
may or may not exercise exclusion clauses similar to the Refugee Convention. As
McAdam has noted, "Its chief function is to provide an alternative basis for eligi-
bility for protection. Understood in this way it does not mandate a lesser duration
or quality of status but simply assesses international protection needs on a wider
basis than the 1951 Convention" (1995, p. 2). As Lord Craighead (noted earlier in
the chapter) suggests, refugee status is worth more than theoretical argument as it
offers increased rights and privileges over other forms of protection status. Forms
of complementary protection have fallen short of mirroring the rights and privileges
of refugee status under the Convention, and the ways in which countries label and
enact complementary protection vary significantly. The EU has issued directives
in relation to member states establishing frameworks for subsidiary protection, but
there is no common status of protection for recipients, therefore enabling differen-
tiation in the status and benefits of those receiving refugee protection and those receiving complementary protection. The United Kingdom requires an asylum claim
to be considered prior to an application for humanitarian protection, which is ordinarily four years. By contrast, Canada operates a system of protection that does
not differentiate between Convention refugees and those who gain complementary
protection. The United States uses a system in which all asylum determination is
considered discretionary and therefore are all regarded as a form of complementary
protection in and of itself, in addition to offering temporary forms of protection and
protection under the *Convention against Torture, and Other Cruel, Inhuman and*

Degrading Treatment or Punishment. However, these different forms of protection carry different entitlements and status. Australia has remained "almost alone" (Hansard, 2009, 8987) among signatory nations in not having a formal system of complementary protection, instead relying on limited, non-compellable discretionary powers of the Minister. Leading international scholar on complementary protection Jane McAdam (2005) has argued that, despite the shortcomings of national complementary protection systems, sufficient standards and obligations are contained in international law to provide legal foundations for domestic complementary protection regimes (p. 18).

Complementary protection has been the focus of advocates seeking to provide women with protection status primarily because Convention status has been so elusive. The legal regulation of refugee determination has so consistently failed women fleeing gender-based persecution, and been so erratic and capricious, that it has been one of the drivers for countries to consider expanded forms of protection. For example, Australia is currently debating legislation to introduce a framework of complementary protection that will bring together refugee protection and Australia's non-refoulement obligations under other treaties within a single integrated protection visa process. In introducing the Bill into the federal parliament the Minister for Immigration specifically identified gender-based persecution as a driver for expanding protection:

> Complementary protection will cover circumstances in which a person may currently be refused a protection visa because the reason for the persecution or harm on return is not one of the specified reasons in the refugee convention—that is, not on the basis of race, religion, nationality, membership of a particular social group or political opinion. For example, it is not certain that a girl who would face a real risk of female genital mutilation would always be covered by the refugee convention, whereas she would be covered under complementary protection. Women at risk of so-called honour killings can also potentially fall through gaps in the refugee convention definition. In some countries victims of rape are executed along with, or rather than, their attackers. Again, depending on the circumstances this situation may not be covered under the refugee convention. The Rudd Labor government is convinced that Australians would expect claims of this gravity, claims involving female genital mutilation, execution for victims of rape and so-called honour killings, to be dealt with through a process that affords natural justice and access to independent merits review. Where such claims are accepted as true, Australians would expect a protection visa to be granted. (Hansard, 2009, 8990)

This view is in stark contrast to the position of the previous Australian Federal Government. The *Khawar* decision, which granted a woman refugee status because of a claim based on domestic violence, was used by the government of the day to introduce legislation to restrict the interpretation of "persecution" within the meaning of s1A(2) of the Convention. The government argued that decisions by the courts and tribunals had expanded the interpretation of the Convention definition beyond what was originally intended. The most damning part of the legislation was that it stipulated that the Convention reason must be the "essential and significant" reason/s identified for the persecution. It was widely understood that this interpretation made it significantly harder for a woman to claim refugee status because decisions granting women status on the basis of gender-based persecution had increasingly relied on quite elaborate and indirect reasoning regarding the "particular social group"/ persecution nexus. The amending legislation introduced a new s 91r into the *Migration Act 1958 (Cth)*. The purpose of this section was to restrict claims of persecution to instances where there was "serious harm" involved.

Following the *Alvarado* case in the United States and decisions in the *Matter of A-T-*, advocates have also argued for legislative guidance for decision-makers in expanding protection grounds which have previously singled out forced abortion and sterilisation but have not included gender-based persecution more broadly. The *Alvarado* case has resulted in extensive pressure on the Obama administration to establish clear legal regulations enabling victims of gender-based persecution to be considered eligible for asylum under the Refugee Convention. For example, a *New York Times* editorial argued:

> The Department of Homeland Security should follow up its brief in the Alvarado case by issuing something more lasting and useful: a firm, clear set of regulations spelling out the conditions under which battered women could be granted asylum here. Such regulations would give invaluable guidance to asylum officials and immigration judges and prevent the years of delays and uncertainty that so worsened Ms Alvarado's ordeal. (9 November 2009)

However, even in the Australian case, the extent to which FGM and honour killings will sit in relation to less titillating forms of harm that women may suffer remains unclear. The use of the above examples in introducing the legislation into the Australian Parliament was about protecting "girls" with predictable processes and outcomes. It is also unclear how the nuances and complexities of gender-based persecution will be understood any differently under a system of complementary protection. We might question whether it is any more likely that a past fear of FGM will suffice for protection or only extend to women who are in fear of being subjected to the practice for the first time.

Adopting complementary protection is, on the one hand, to be applauded, for it makes possible protection for those not originally envisaged as requiring protection under the Refugee Convention; yet, on the other hand, it has the potential to encapsulate a lower level of rights and privileges.

In relation to gender-based violence the regulatory edifice has been erratic and unreliable. As Soler and Musao have urged, in the United States "[i]t's time we put our regulatory house in order and assured victims of gender based violence that they can count on justice…if federal agencies don't do it through regulation, it's time for Congress to do it through legislation" (Soler & Musalo, July 18, 2008, *The Washington Post*).

11   Conclusion

One of the many reasons why women cross borders in extra legal ways is that they need international legal protection. There is a nascent body of social science literature that demonstrates that crossing borders illegally is not an equally available option. For example:

There are many practical reasons why the number of women asylum seekers remains so low. First, women who would have legitimate claims for asylum often come from countries where they have few or no rights, which limits their ability to leave their countries in search of protection. Second, they are frequently—if not always—primary caretakers for their children and extended family. Thus they often have to choose between leaving family behind, or exposing them to the risks of travel to the potential country of refuge. Finally, women asylum seekers often have little control over family resources, making it impossible for them to have the means to travel to a country where they might seek asylum. (Musalo, 2008)

Refugee determination is a regulatory mechanism of the territorial sovereignty of the nation-state, and hence its discursive manoeuvring can be said to both respond to and shape the conditions of the border for women seeking to extra-legally cross into the Global North. However, when women have sought protection because of gender-based persecution their cases have been cast as the vanguard of a potential flood of women across borders. For example, those seeking justice can be thwarted by the discourse into which they must enter and from which they must emerge in a particular and acceptable form (or stand to be effectively "othered" and hence diminished). In recognising refugee status, the experience of persecution and the reasons for that persecution come to be absorbed into the master narrative. In the Australian context, this master narrative is the legal discourse of the RRT, not that of the woman before it. The RRT, as a bulwark of the determination process prescribed by the Australian Government, recognises experiences and meanings only if they are first usurped by the master narrative of the determination process. As Foucault and Fairclough have argued, legal discourses can alert us to both the micro and macro operations of (gendered) power. Indeed, the gendered ideological work of the Tribunal can be read, at least in part, through its written decisions. Such ideological work is not always smooth or without contradiction, but it did point to the important role gender plays in policies of exclusion and the ways in which exclusion is discursively played out on women who seek protection. This in turn raises questions about the extent to which engaging with the law around crimes of sexual violence is a productive process.

Laws are meaningless until they are put into practice by judicial interpretation in the context of legal proceedings (Pether & Threadgold, 2000). Consequently, we need to come to terms with the ways in which we can insist that formal legal rationality, as found in legal discourse, not demarcate and sanction the experience of the woman standing before it. Legal narratives do not and cannot comprehend the complexity of gender-based persecution. In so doing we can begin to find alternative ways, and alternative grounds, for women to mount gender-based persecution claims to refugee status. It may be that the enumerated ground "political opinion" holds significantly greater scope for addressing the concerns raised in the cases canvassed in this chapter. At the same time, it is recognised that even the most dynamic interpretations of politics will always, and by necessity, fall short. This is because we continue to look to the legal as an answer to the social, the political and the cultural, and invest new and greater powers in the state enforcement machinery and the refugee determination procedure (in this case of the RRT) as the primary legitimating discourse. Even when women achieve refugee status (justice) by utilising the ground "particular social group", the process by which such justice is accessed, through legal discourse, currently reinforces dominant (colonial) racial and patriarchal values.

Gender-based persecution, when approached via the enumerated ground "particular social group", is thereby diminished and denied in a range of ways. Mostly this has assumed the form of what Cohen (2001) has described as interpretive denial. Yet literal and legal denial is also at work. All three forms of denial in turn have worked to assure an overall denial of responsibility on the part of the RRT in acknowledging gender-based persecution as a (personal) political and legal experience. Such denial draws heavily on the gendered ideological work of the RRT to distance gender-based persecution from refugee protection administered by the nation-state.

12   Summary

This chapter considers the ways in which law, particularly refugee law, contributes to the repudiation of women's experiences of gender-based violence as a driver of forced migration. A lack of legal status keeps people in a transient state—it keeps them in a legal frontier land, a border region where they are not recognised as equal or deserving and subject to unpredictable consequences. Asylum law requires legally recognisable, chronologically acceptable periods of transit and engagement in the asylum process which the process of fleeing persecution and conflict rarely enable. This chapter considers asylum and gender-based persecution in the United States, United Kingdom and Australia.

Chapter 5
Policing the Border Within: Sex Trafficking and the Regulation of Sex Work

...the claims being made about the wide extent of sex trafficking cannot be substantiated....
(Minister for Immigration and Multicultural and Indigenous Affairs, 1 April 2003, Press Release)

The illegal international trade in people has been growing considerably in recent years. Australia will not tolerate this repugnant trade which deals with women and children in a sexually exploitative manner. Today we are announcing a comprehensive strategy to fight this insidious crime.
(Minister for Justice and Customs, 13 October 2003a)

...evidence in this field is scanty....
(Judy Maddigan, MP Chair of the Victorian Parliamentary Inquiry into Trafficking for Sex Work, June 2010)

The rhetoric and the policy in relation to human trafficking has largely been located within the broader domain of counter–organised crime measures and the primary criminal justice focus has been directed at crimes that involve the breaching of borders and migration law. In practice this is increasingly realised through increased scrutiny of the sex industry and has involved attempts at recriminalising sex work by stealth. It has done so at the expense of more complex and inter-industry analysis of trafficking practices—not just sex trafficking (cf. Hathaway, 2008). Weber (2006) has posited that borders are mobile and increasingly personally mobile—that is, borders are being attached to individuals rather than to specific places or sites. Thus, the border that requires policing morphs into a person that requires policing. This chapter suggests that the focus on policing sex trafficking is primarily concerned with the breach of the border, and is increasingly policed within countries and on the bodies of women who legitimately work in the sex industry.

This chapter was co-authored with Marie Segrave, Monash University.

S. Pickering, *Women, Borders, and Violence,*
DOI 10.1007/978-1-4419-0271-9_5, © Springer Science+Business Media, LLC 2011

This chapter examines the background to the issue of the trafficking of women into sexual servitude in the Australian context. The nature and extent of trafficking will be briefly explored, followed by a presentation of the legislative approaches to the criminalisation of trafficking-related offences. An overview of some of the key factors contributing to the development of the Australian anti-trafficking package will precede an outline of the package itself, followed by an exploration of some of the main criticisms and concerns raised in response to this new approach. The chapter will then posit alternative transnational frameworks within which sex trafficking needs to be understood if responses other than criminalisation of the sex industry are to be made possible.

In 2003, the Australian Government shifted from a firm stance maintaining that the trafficking of women into the sex industry in Australia was not a large-scale problem (evidenced by the lack of victims identifying themselves to government officials) to a Australian $20-million commitment to a national anti-trafficking package. A number of factors culminated in the government's shift in direction, including the momentum of public discussion generated by persistent media coverage of the issue throughout 2003, and international pressure on the government to take trafficking seriously and to implement initiatives to address it. Critics contend that the package has achieved the central aim of ensuring that the government is seen to be actively pursuing the trafficking of people into Australia, particularly the trafficking of women into sexual servitude, without fundamentally shifting from a traditional law and order approach to identifying, understanding and responding to the issues surrounding trafficking in Australia (cf. Segrave, Milivojevic, & Pickering, 2009).

The government's package became a central plank in increasing the national security profile of the Australian Federal Police (AFP) and expanding its policing remit to include various national security issues—from terrorism to people smuggling and sex trafficking. As a result, trafficking was explained primarily as a crime that involved both the exploitation of individuals *and* the breach of migration law, as offenders were involved in profit from the exploitation of those who they assisted to cross borders. The policy and policing rhetoric was concerned with criminal networks that were implicitly acknowledged to be ethnically identifiable and linked to other illicit cross-border activity (most usually drugs). This echoed international commitments to address human trafficking embodied in the *Protocol to Prevent, Suppress and Punish Trafficking in Persons, especially Women and Children* one of three protocols under the *UN Convention against Transnational Organized Crime*. The Convention was (and is) upheld as

a major step forward in the fight against transnational organized crime…signif[ying] the recognition by Member States of the seriousness of the problems posed by it [and their] commit[ment]…to taking a series of measures against transnational organized crime, including the creation of domestic criminal offence…; the adoption of new and sweeping frameworks for extradition, mutual legal assistance and law enforcement cooperation; and the promotion of training and technical assistance for building or upgrading the necessary capacity of national authorities. (UNODC, 2010b)

1 The Nature and Extent of the Trafficking of Women into Sexual Servitude in Australia

The Government treats the issues of people trafficking in the sex industry with a high priority and while numbers involved appear to be low, operational activities will continue both within Australia and overseas to bring this industry to an end. (Minister for Immigration and Multicultural and Indigenous Affairs, 1 April 2003)

Given the illicit nature of people trafficking—that it is both illegal and transnational—there are many difficulties faced in accurately identify the size and scale of trafficking, both internationally and within Australia (Segrave et al., 2009; Makkai, 2003, p. 3). These difficulties include a lack of accurate statistical data, particularly the absence of a systematic data collection process and the fact that the identification of people trafficking relies primarily on women identifying themselves to authorities (Carrington & Hearn, 2003, p. 5; also Makkai, 2003). Yet the nature of trafficking is such that many factors inhibit women from coming forward, and underreporting is therefore a significant issue. Factors such as language barriers, mistrust of authorities, fear of reprisals, an inability to move freely to access assistance or seek help, and the complex reasons why trafficked victims may not actually want to be identified or "rescued" all contribute to the non-reporting of trafficking. Despite the difficulties in gathering data and extrapolating accurate figures from the data, stakeholders (including governments and non-government organisations) routinely estimate prevalence levels based on data from various sources, ranging from official crime- and migration-related statistics to anecdotal information from key informants. As a result, there is often disparity in the reported levels at both the international and national levels and between estimates provided by different organisations (Segrave et al., 2009; Makkai, 2003, p. 8).

In Australia the estimates have ranged from 1,000 women in Australia working in sexual servitude (Roxon, Maltzahn, & Costello, 2004, p. 3) to AFP estimates of less than one hundred (Lawler in JCACC, 2004b, p. 4). The federal government relies on the data provided by police and immigration authorities to support its official stance that while trafficking does exist in Australia the actual incidence is low:

[Between 1 July 2002 and 28 February 2003] immigration compliance staff located 134 people working illegally in the sex industry. Of those located, four women have made complaints about trafficking—that is, they stated they were brought to Australia under false pretences by unscrupulous individuals for the express purpose of forcing them into a form of sexual slavery. (Minister for Immigration and Multicultural and Indigenous Affairs, 1 April 2003)

The data that has been produced most recently point to the potentially untapped reality of labour exploitation outside the sex industry that has to date been largely ignored by counter-trafficking efforts in Australia (see Segrave, 2009). Of those trafficked into the sex industry, the majority tend to be aware that they will be engaged in some form of sex work but are deceived as to the nature of the contract and the conditions under which they will be working (Maltzahn, 2004). In Australia women tend to have come from nations within the South-East Asian region and in smaller numbers from Europe and Latin America (McKinney in JCACC, 2004a, p. 37; Maltzahn, 2004). Most women trafficked into Australia will leave the country through contact with the Department of Immigration, having made little, if any, money, and authorities remaining unaware of how the women came to be in Australia or the victimisation they experienced while in the country. Reports indicate that women trafficked into Australia are subjected to numerous human rights abuses, which until recently was an unacknowledged aspect of trafficking (Roxon et al., 2004).

2   Trafficking into the Sex Industry in Australian Law

Prior to 1999, no specific legislative framework existed to protect victims of trafficking or to pursue those involved in the trafficking of women into sexual servitude. The Australian Law Reform Commission in the early 1990s made recommendations that the federal criminal code slavery laws be updated however, no action was taken. In the late 1990s "sex slavery" cases began to receive some attention. One high-profile Victorian case *Queen vs Gary Glazner 2000* highlighted the limited options available to prosecute trafficking-related offences (see Ford, 2001). Glazner was charged for offences pertaining to breaches of state prostitution regulation laws (specifically the *Prostitution Control Act (VIC)* 1994).

In the late 1990s an examination of the Commonwealth Government's proposal to enact laws dealing with slavery and sexual servitude resulted in the introduction of the *Criminal Code Amendment (Slavery and Sexual Servitude) Act* in 1999 (Norberry & Guest, 1999, p. 2). Rather than identifying a specific "trafficking in persons" offence, the legislation identified three separate trafficking-related offences—slavery, sexual servitude and deceptive recruiting—but it did not refer specifically to human trafficking as an offence. Despite the introduction of this legislation, anecdotal reports indicated that even with legislation to pursue these offences, the prosecution of individuals involved in the trafficking of women into the sex industry were only successful through minor offences relating to migration and prostitution legislation (Payne, 2003, p. 4).

In late 2003, however, a number of developments significantly changed the Australian anti-trafficking landscape. From an issue ignored by authorities and effectively denied by policy makers, in October 2003 it was brought to the fore as a critical and urgent national concern. The factors contributing to this dramatic shift are detailed below, but it is worth noting that when trafficking was engaged as a national concern the response was located within the broader transnational crime framework within which people smuggling was already firmly ensconced. Thus, it officially placed trafficking within the remit of border control and the criminal justice system. Although reference to human rights and humanitarian issues has been made in relation to the experiences of trafficked women, the "real" work in relation to people trafficking has centred on the prosecution of traffickers, the operation of border controls and attempts by immigration authorities to locate victims.

3   Catalysts to Change: Factors Contributing to the Development of the Anti-Trafficking Package

The development of a Commonwealth package to address trafficking was the culmination of pressures and influence at the national and international level, some of which was played out in the public realm, while some unfolded behind closed doors. It is not possible to identify the full range of factors that contributed to the government's decision to develop this package, yet a number of key factors can be identified that placed pressure on the Australian Government to acknowledge that trafficking is a problem in Australia, and to reassess existing approaches.

3.1   International Recognition: Raising the Standard

The United Nations *Convention against Transnational Organized Crime* (the Convention) was adopted at the fifty-fifth session of the General Assembly of the UN on 15 November 2002. Supplementary to the Convention were three Protocols, one of which was the *Protocol to Prevent, Suppress and Punish Trafficking in Persons, especially Women and Children* (the Trafficking Protocol). The Trafficking Protocol identifies all trafficked persons, particularly women in prostitution and child labourers, as victims of crime. It recognises the need for all victims of trafficking to be protected and shifts the burden of proof away from victims such that consent is no longer relevant because "the key actionable element in the trafficking process is exploitation" (Raymond, 2002, p. 495). However, as Goodey (2003, p. 423) notes, while this initiative may be "laudable, there is no sense of [its] practicality", particularly in terms of the Trafficking Protocol's requirement that state parties adopt measures to address and alleviate factors that contribute to the trafficking of people, including poverty, low economic development and lack of equal opportunities. The Trafficking Protocol was most significant for reconceptualising people trafficking within a human rights framework and, more importantly, for providing "a comprehensive legal framework to guide national governments' response to organised crime and to facilitate greater international cooperation between States" (Carrington & Hearn, 2003, p. 7).

Both the Convention and the Trafficking Protocol were opened for signature on 13 December 2000, and although Australia signed the Convention as soon as it opened for signature, the signing of the Trafficking Protocol was delayed until 11 December 2002. Reflecting the border control policy focus at the time, Australia signed the Trafficking Protocol with the condition that "nothing in the Protocol shall be seen to be imposing obligations on Australia to admit or retain within its borders persons in respect of whom Australia would otherwise have an obligation to admit or retain within its borders" (UNODC, 2004). Nonetheless, signing of the Trafficking Protocol placed pressure on the Australian Government to redevelop Commonwealth legislation to reflect the definition in the Trafficking Protocol and its emphasis on victim support.

3.2   *International Pressure*

Around the same period as the Trafficking Protocol was moving towards finalisation, the United States appointed itself the "global sheriff" on counter-trafficking (Chuang, 2006). The development of a legislative and administrative regime in the United States to monitor and assess national and international measures to address this issue has significantly influenced the counter-trafficking landscape in terms of the uptake of national commitments to address the issue and the parameters of count-trafficking policies (Cheung, 2006).

The US Department of State established the Office to Monitor and Combat Trafficking in Persons in October 2001, a body committed primarily to annually producing a report that reviews and ranks countries' efforts to address trafficking according to US-defined minimum standards (USDOS, 2010). The review and assessment process is given weight by the informal diplomatic weight of US pressure and through the legislated sanctions regime which authorises the withdrawal of financial assistance (excluding trade-related and humanitarian assistance) from countries that fail to comply and show no signs of addressing this failure (USDOS, 2002, p. 10).

US pressure on the Australian Government to reassess its national approach to trafficking policy has been noted as a key driver of the government's reassessment of the priority given to people trafficking in Australia, particularly the trafficking of women into sexual servitude. Australian media reports around that time revealed that US State Department officials had begun to ask difficult questions regarding the extent of trafficking in Australia, placing pressure on the Australian Government to respond by developing a new policy (Alcorn & Minchin, 2003). A number of sources confirmed that Australia risked being named and criticised by the US State Department report if its attitude did not change (Alcorn & Minchin, 2003). In early 2003 the Australian Government had no trafficking-specific policy. It is worth noting that the policy was introduced in late 2003 and the first Australian inclusion in the TIP Report occurred in 2004, for which Australia received a Tier One ranking—the best ranking possible in the reporting system (USDOS, 2004).

3.3   *Limitations of the National Legislation*

Despite the significance of the *Criminal Code Amendment (Slavery and Sexual Servitude) Act 1999* in acknowledging trafficking into sexual servitude as a criminal offence, it was the subject of some criticism, particularly in relation to the lack of prosecutions made under these laws. Between the introduction of the legislation on 24 March 1999 and 26 February 2004, the AFP conducted 62 investigations into offences identified within this legislation (of which 15 were underway in February 2004) and have laid 35 charges (Joint Committee on the ACC, Proof Committee Hansard, 26 February 2004, p. 3). None successfully progressed through Australian courts; thus, at the time it was concluded that "the effective prosecution of traffickers is something that eludes Australia" (Iselin, 2003, p. 2).

The legislation was focused upon traffickers with little regard for the needs of victims, such that the legal framework ensured that victims were regarded predominantly as "evidence"—considered only within the context of the investigation and court proceedings, with little regard for victims' lives and welfare outside the legal system. Such a framework can be considered counterproductive:

> The successful prosecution of traffickers relies on the cooperation of the victims of traffickers, who without mandated support, protection or means of redress are unlikely to cooperate with law enforcement agencies.... The unintended consequence is that traffickers escape prosecution while trafficking victims are detained in inappropriate conditions, put at risk of being returned to an unsafe environment and exposed to possible revictimisation. (Carrington & Hearn, 2003, p. 1)

A further concern with the legislation at the time was narrow offence definitions. The offence of "deceptive recruiting", for example, applied only to cases where a person is deceived about the nature of the work not those who agree to work in the sex industry but are deceived about the *conditions* of that work (Carrington & Hearn, 2003, p. 9). This framework meant that the majority of reported cases of trafficking into sexual servitude, which involved women who agreed to work in the sex industry but not to the exploitative conditions of work, were not entitled to protection under Australian legislation (Maltzahn, 2004). Thus, the definitions came under increased scrutiny for lacking an appreciation of contemporary trafficking practices and the experiences of trafficked women, resulting in legislation that is limited and narrow in its applicability (Maltzahn, 2003, p. 21; Costello in JCACC, 2003, p. 35).

Finally, the trafficking of women into the sex industry crosses a complex legal terrain of legislation and law enforcement boundaries. Immigration law, Commonwealth slavery and sexual servitude laws, state and territory sexual servitude laws, and local government regulations may all be implicated in the identification of women trafficked into sexual servitude and the pursuit of a range of charges against those involved in trafficking. This translated into a situation in Australia where trafficking-related issues were a concern for multiple agencies yet no agency specifically had the responsibility for or the capacity to coordinate activities. As international pressure mounted on Australia's response to trafficking, it became increasingly evident that the existing legislative framework was an effective measure to address the trafficking of women into sexual servitude in Australia. The international pressure combined with media maelstrom that developed over 2002 and 2003 (see Carrington & Hearn, 2003, p. 13) played a significant role in the 2003 federal turnaround on human trafficking.

4 The National Response

On 13 October 2003, a joint ministerial media release announced the federal government's "commitment to combating the repugnant trade of trafficking in people" in the form of a four-year, Australian $20-million anti-trafficking package to "combat this growing form of transnational organised crime" (Attorney-General,

13 October 2003). The central focus of the package was to enhance the detection, investigation and prosecution of traffickers, but it also demonstrated a marked shift in the identification of victims' needs. In addition to the criminal justice provisions, the package outlined the development of a range of services to support victims as well as efforts in countries of origin (specifically Thailand) to work towards the prevention of trafficking of persons. The package identified the introduction of a number of initiatives under the *Commonwealth Action Plan to Eradicate Trafficking in Persons.*

The policy package was "designed to focus on the full cycle of trafficking from recruitment to reintegration and to give equal weight to the three critical areas of prevention, prosecution and victim support" (Blackburn in JCACC, 2004b, p. 14). However, the distribution of funding was indicative of a "crime-fighting" emphasis within the package with the real investment—that is, the area receiving the majority of the funding—channelled to enhancing the policing, investigation and enforcement of trafficking legislation.

In June 2003 a Federal Parliamentary Joint Committee on the Australian Crime Commission was established to conduct an inquiry into the trafficking of women for sexual servitude. The Committee Process (including written submissions and public hearings) was conducted in late 2003 and early 2004 and was able to capture some insight into the early implementation of the newly established policy response. Observing the implementation of the process, a number of stakeholders criticized the policy framework, key elements of the package and implementation dilemmas and limitations.

Key early concerns included the delay in implementing key aspects of the package—while policing initiatives were established within months (see Lawler in JCACC, 2004b), new legislation was slow to be developed and the victim support program took over six months to become operational and was then limited in terms of the support provided (Roxon et al., 2004, p. 5).

Immediately upon implementation it became clear that the issue of the migration status of victims created complex immigration and criminal justice tensions. The importance of appropriate visa arrangements that are easily accessible and amenable to the individual circumstances of those accessing them has been recognised both internationally and nationally, and viewed as an essential aspect of the successful prosecution of offenders. The Australian anti-trafficking package promised the introduction of new arrangements which resulted in the creation of a bridging (F) visa that entitles all victims of trafficking to a 30-day visa:

> The intensive support package is available for the first 30 days to all victims of trafficking, specifically to enable the victims the time and space to determine whether they wish to cooperate with law enforcement agencies. (Blackburn in JCACC, 2004b, p. 25)

Following this 30-day period, if a person is willing and able to assist law enforcement agencies, the new criminal justice stay visa framework (specifically the new witness protection visa) is utilised (which an agency such as the AFP applies for on behalf of the victim), which guarantees the continuation of comprehensive support for the victim. However:

> If the person is not willing and able to assist law enforcement agencies, the new visa arrangements do not apply, [and] they are dealt with under existing arrangements under the Immigration Act. (Blackburn, JCACC, 2004b, p. 25)

These new arrangements were the subject of much discussion and criticism, both during the inquiry and in other arenas later, primarily concerning the conditional nature of the arrangements such that women are placed "in a position where they must choose between support and involvement in investigation and testifying, or nothing" (Roxon et al., 2004, p. 5). Critically, there was no guarantee of any long-term support including access to a long-term visa beyond the criminal justice process. Thus, despite the provision of new visa regulations, and the demands placed on women to assist with criminal cases as they progressed through the criminal justice system, their long-term status within Australia regardless of the level of assistance they provide to authorities remained at all times uncertain.

The rhetoric surrounding the announcement of this anti-trafficking package proclaimed the Australian Government's commitment to combat trafficking. If we fast forward from the original policy to the current state of counter-trafficking efforts in Australia, we track how this has developed over time.

4.1 The Contemporary Situation in Australia

Since 2004, Australia has consistently been rated as "Tier One" nation in the US TIP Report (USDOS, 2004, 2005, 2006, 2007, 2008, 2009, 2010). There have been some changes over time including amended visa processes, the altering of some aspects of victim support provisions and in 2005 the introduction of the *Criminal Code Amendment (Trafficking in Persons Offences) Act 2005* with specific offences that criminalise trafficking in persons activity. These elements and the policy framework as a whole have been the subject of ongoing discussion and critique (see Pearson, 2007; Burn et al., 2005; Burn & Simmons, 2005; Segrave & Milivojevic, 2005; Burn et al., 2006; McSherry, 2007). However, despite the lack of any comprehensive analysis of the implementation and impact of the policy response as a whole the federal government made a commitment in 2007 to "build on the success of the existing initiatives" (Attorney-General's Department, 2007a) dedicating a further Australian $38.3 million over four years to the counter-trafficking policy strategy (ANAO, 2009, p. 11).

The only significant report related to the policy response was published in 2009 by the Australian National Audit Office (ANAO) when it tabled its report on the *Management of the Australian Government's Action Plan to Eradicate Trafficking in Persons* (ANAO, 2009). The report came about from the 2004 *Parliamentary Joint Committee on the Australian Crime Commission's* recommendation that an audit be conducted into the management of the policy response (ANAO, 2009, p. 13). However, the mandate of this review was specifically to assess the inter-government arrangements in relation first to monitoring the contributions of the various agencies to the achievement of the outcomes of the policy[1] and second to assessing whether the measures in place effectively manage, monitor and assess performance (ANAO, 2009, p. 13). This report highlighted significant failures in the implementation of the policy. These failures includes the miscommunication between Immigration and Policing authorities (ANAO, 2009, pp. 18–19) and the tendency for implementation of measures to be reported as a "success" despite the lack of evidence of a range of measures to effectively reduce the number of people being exploited (ANAO, 2009, pp. 18–19). Given its mandate the scope of the recommendations of the ANAO report were limited, but called for greater transparency and reporting of practices. The outcome of this call was the publishing of the 2009 inaugural Anti–People Trafficking Interdepartmental Committee (APTIC) report on the Australian response to trafficking in persons, which was noted as a vital part of "monitoring and measuring progress of the anti–people trafficking strategy" to "ensure Australia's success in combating this crime" (APTIC, 2009, p. iii). This report produce process and trend data from the various agencies involved in implementing the response and is not linked to any formal process of evaluation (see Segrave & Milivojevic, in press).

The data published in the 2009 APTIC report do reveal, however, that despite the millions of dollars and resources dedicated to this issue, the politically salient and desired criminal justice outcomes are rare indeed. The report states that "between January 2004 and April 2009, the Australian Federal Police undertook over 270 investigations and assessments of allegations of trafficking-related offences, leading to 34 people being charged and seven convictions", with "five trafficking related matters before the Australian courts" (APTIC, 2009, p. iii). The ongoing challenges and limits of the criminal justice–oriented counter-trafficking model revealed in these data not unique to Australia (see USDOS, 2010), suggesting that it is the assumptions and priorities underpinning the transnational organised crime model that require closer examination and critique. Yet, what we have witnessed most recently in one state of Australia, Victoria, is the continuation of poorly informed political agendas driving discussions about and responses to human trafficking that are further entrenching problematic and ineffective policy models.

4.2   State-Level Intervention

Up until very recently human trafficking, as a form of transnational crime, was embraced by the federal government as a national concern and the response to the issue had been developed at the national level, to be implemented by national agencies across Australia. However, in 2009 the Australian approach to sex trafficking expe-

---

[1] Specifically the Attorney-General's Department (AGD), the Department of Immigration & Citizenship (DIAC), the Australian Federal Police (AFP) and the Department of Families, Housing, Community Services & Indigenous Affairs (FACSIA) within which the Office for Women (OfW) is currently located.

rienced an unpredicted intervention. The Victorian Parliament announced its own Inquiry into Trafficking into the Sex Industry. Victoria has had a decriminalised sex industry since 2006, when, following the *Neave Report*, it took a harm minimisation approach to sex work. This inquiry was unusual because up until that time trafficking had been considered a federal issue to be tackled nationally across all states and territories and responded to primarily by the AFP, in conjunction with a range of other federal agencies including the Department of Immigration. It was also unusual as it effectively ignored the international recognition of the need to address all forms of human trafficking, returning to the much-criticised focus on sex trafficking. Through its terms of reference the Inquiry reunited the connection between human trafficking, sex work and sex industry regulation in a way that national and international advocates have successfully critiqued and challenged (Ditmore & Wijers, 2003; Saunders & Soderlund, 2003; Kapur, 2005).

In its *Final Report of the Inquiry into People Trafficking for Sex Work*, the state-based approach to sex trafficking was justified with the following statements:

> The majority of Victorians would be horrified if they knew that women are trafficked to Australia for sexual purposes.... This report is perhaps an early step in making the community aware of this crime and instituting a better regime to protect these vulnerable women. Whilst immigration is covered by the Federal jurisdiction, the women are employed in Victoria and rely on the support of the Victorian community and Government for protection. (Maddigan, 2010, p. iii)

The Victorian Parliamentary Inquiry did not have the clout of a "Government Inquiry" —the report is tabled in Parliament and the response may be the adoption of all or none of its recommendations. The Report ran to some 257 pages and included 27 recommendations. What is most notable is that the various recommendations included significant duplication of Commonwealth legislation and policing as well as broader support and education platforms. The difference between the Report and the existing federal framework was that it proposed a series of initiatives that would effectively recriminalise the legitimate sex industry in Victoria and give anti-prostitution NGOs considerable political and material resources in the process. The Inquiry effectively refocused the issue of trafficking as one primarily to do with prostitution rather than one concerned with migration and human rights.

The Chair of the Inquiry acknowledged that the submissions made to the Committee revealed that evidence on sex trafficking is "scanty"—an unfortunate error which set the tone for a document that was primarily focused on sex rather than harm. Reflecting this view and despite the very limited data, the Committee made recommendations that involved specific resource development in Victoria, including Victoria Police anti-trafficking initiatives, the introduction of a state-based offence of debt bondage, the substantial financing of Victorian-based NGOs and the development of state-based victim support measures.

There is little justification for the recommendations evidenced within the Report. Indeed, the Report recommendations suggest that Victorian and national authorities and departments will address the issues. The proposals, however risk legislative, enforcement and resource confusion and at worst play into opportunistic law and order politics.

A central component of the recommendations was the reliance on the criminal justice system as the primary mechanism for identifying and responding to sex trafficking, consistent with the national approach adopted seven years earlier still in place. Those responsible for developing the recommendations effectively evaded the key messages from recent Australian data (cited in the literature review of the report) which indicate that the criminal justice system, despite significant resourcing in recent years, has not been able to meaningfully translate investigations into convictions (Segrave et al., 2009). More importantly, the recommendations did not engage with the burgeoning recognition that human trafficking must be considered within the broader scope of labour migration and exploitation (see Segrave, 2008). The recommendations fail to challenge nations such as Australia to recognise the rights of migrant men and women engaged in any work, including sex work, and to earn a living with fair and equitable terms of employment in which they are fairly remunerated for their labour. Focusing on creating a regulatory environment that includes more meaningful engagement with workers in terms of the minimisation of harm and the enhancement of worker autonomy would have long-term benefits. Instead the report promotes increased regulation of the sex industry to seek out victims of trafficking and the promotion of NGOs as key players in this process—an approach that has the potential to amplify rather than ameliorate the social stigma that often surrounds sex work which can further impede those who may wish to receive or seek out some form of assistance.

5 Processes of Globalisation and Circuits of Survival

Discourses of victimisation have shaped public debate around sex trafficking in Australia. This coverage has largely erased the role of the state beyond criminalisation processes. While predominant discourses shaping the debate on sex trafficking prioritise explanations of organised crime and women's violent victimisation, the "common-sense" response will remain an escalation in law enforcement. Such a narrow response silences the challenges to sovereignty and boundary transgression that sex trafficking may constitute, and silences the conditions under which women migrate and work. Instead we need to understand sex trafficking within frames of migration and globalisation rather than criminalisation and victimisation. This is not to suggest that migration and globalisation ignore the victim's experiences, but rather they refuse to understand sex trafficking within narrow parameters of prostitution and law enforcement. By championing criminalisation policies the state comes to occupy a central role in responding to the practice without consideration of how the state contributes to its maintenance: through its participation in global systems and through practices of statecraft.

Sex trafficking cannot be understood apart from a range of services women provide both within and outside the "family" as poorly paid and unskilled workers in agricultural, domestic and factory spheres that now have international markets. No longer bound to the nation-state, such work now crosses borders as part of the transnational flow of labour: "In this international demand for female services, supply follows closely behind and women often migrate to provide their services to an international clientele" (Coomaraswamy, 2003, p. 21). We need to develop an understanding of sex trafficking that considered the multiple reasons why women seek to migrate and the processes of globalisation that now define patterns of migration. As Coomaraswamy states: "Trafficking must be seen in the context of migration and migration patterns" (Coomaraswamy, 2003, p. 22). Sassen (2000) argues that we must understand the role of broader economic trends that inform sex trafficking—particularly between the Global North and the Global South in relation to national debt, free trade zones and the Global North's insatiable desire for cheap Southern labour:

> The employment or use of foreign-born women covers an increasingly broad range of economic sectors, some in highly regulated industries, such as nursing, and some illegal and illicit, such as prostitution. These circuits could be considered as indicators of the (albeit partial) feminization of survival, because it is increasingly on the backs of women that these forms of making a living, earning a profit and securing government revenue are realized. (Sassen, 2002, p. 506)

Sassen (2000) has further argued that we can now trace counter geographies of globalisation in which we see women pursuing circuits of survival that can simultaneously disempower them at the hands of abusive traffickers while also empowering them as alternative legal and social subjects. No such tracing has been undertaken by Australian feminists or advocates. As a result, sex trafficking in Australia has remained primarily an issue of prostitution.

6   Role of the State: Boundary Inscription Practices

Despite it not being discussed as a migration issue, sex trafficking into Australia has nonetheless been subject to the repressive discourses of border protection that dominate current punitive Australian approaches to asylum seekers and refugees. Without any of the benefits that would come were sex trafficking to be understood as a broader migration issue (and the consequent reshaping of debate and response), those who are trafficked have become another target of the complex border inscription practices that many state and non-state agencies now perform in Australia.

Through national institutions, such as the AFP, and to a lesser extent state police services, the criminalisation of trafficking can be viewed as an important site wherein the state defines itself through its inclusion and exclusion of others. As such, it draws on a familiar and convincing narrative of the deviancy of those who come to Australia seeking refugee protection (Pickering, 2001). Despite having the frame of international refugee protection, asylum seekers have largely been considered "illegal", and concomitantly Australia seeks to deter, detect and detain those who attempt to disrupt its sovereign integrity of its borders. Sex trafficking has been inserted into a public debate in which legislatures and community leaders have been quick to identify women trafficked for sex as victims, but slow to identify Australia's role in the global production of conditions under which women are trafficked. As a result, sex trafficking has primarily fallen within the remit of law enforcement and been considered a problem that can be policed out—much like the refugee can be policed out of ever claiming Australia's protection.

Australia's approach to sex trafficking was brought into crisis when a woman trafficked to Australia successfully claimed refugee status. The woman had been trafficked from Burma through Thailand and onto Australia. She was without effective state protection in both Burma and Thailand, and had experienced persecution in both countries. The decision in February 2003 to approve her claim for refugee status sent some important messages that resonate with both Coomaraswamy's and Sassen's scholarship: first, the determination acknowledges that women who are trafficked can become alternative legal actors who challenge the trans-state system; second, it recognises the persecution women suffer in both sending and receiving countries; third, it identifies the need for a protection solution that is grounded in migration status; and fourth, it locates this protection and migration solution within a broader human rights frame that brings both sending and receiving counties to heel by taking the determination of a woman's future out of state hands and returning it to international processes of, in this case, refugee determination. No longer is sex trafficking a matter of poverty, prostitution or law enforcement. It is about human rights, women's empowerment and transnational protection.

7   Conclusion

Sex trafficking has become yet another site for the enforcement of borders, particularly through the familiar discourses and actions of criminal justice. This occurs in the absence of discussions of globalisation or alternative readings of migration that understand women's experiences of sex trafficking as constituent parts of feminised circuits of survival that exist in our world. Understanding sex trafficking primarily as an issue of migration under conditions of globalisation unlocks sex trafficking from a stifling and rigid debate on prostitution and law enforcement.

8   Summary

The rhetoric and the policy in relation to human trafficking has been located within the broader domain of counter–organised crime measures and the primary criminal justice focus has been directed at crimes that involve the breaching of borders. In practice this is increasingly realised through increased scrutiny of the sex industry and has involved attempts at recriminalising sex work by stealth. It has done so at the expense of more complex and inter-industry analysis of trafficking practices—not just sex trafficking. Weber (2006) has posited that borders are mobile and increasingly personally mobile—that is, borders are being attached to individuals rather than to specific places or sites. Thus, the border that requires policing morphs into a person that requires policing. This chapter argues that the focus on policing sex trafficking as a crime is primarily concerned with the breach of the border, and is increasingly policed within countries and on the bodies of women who legitimately work in the sex industry.

Chapter 6
Women, Borders, and Violence

Borders are of central concern to criminologists because of the concentration of political and material resources mobilised in their "defence", for the physical exclusion of people and for their signifying role in the enactment of legal and social processes aimed at identifying people as illegal. The effective "illegalisation" of migration that Dauvergne (2008) elegantly outlines in her work on making people illegal has been centred on border control imperatives that operate in symbiotic relationship with moral panics around unregulated migration flows. Yet it is not migration in its entirety that has fuelled such concerns but rather the unregulated migratory flows that run from the Global South to the Global North (Young, 2007). The escalation of regulatory efforts against extra legal migration has taken on domestic and international significance at the same time that "illegal" has become a noun used to describe people rather than their actions (Bacon, 2007). This has occurred largely because of a range of factors mostly attributed to globalisation, but which have significant historical antecedents around identity and sovereignty as well as political expediencies around performances of effective government. In many ways this book takes much of this scholarship for granted. It does so in order to ask the question: what are women's experiences of policing when they cross borders extra legally? The answer has overwhelmingly focused on the complex interplay between state and non-state agents, operating in formal and informal contexts. It has done so by mapping the nonlinear journeys of women to and through global frontier lands between the Global North and Global South. While it charts their many vulnerabilities, particularly in relation to sexual and gender-based violence and political community, it also identifies points of resistance, albeit often of a limited kind. In this chapter I try to draw together the strands of arguments offered in the preceding chapters and consider some of the implications for criminology.

It is perhaps unsurprising that a book focused on women's accounts of gendered violence produce non-state-based views of violence, migration and security. As Shepherd has noted, "...studying the subjects produced through gendered violence in the context of debates over the meaning and content of security provides more coherent accounts of both violence and security" (2007, p. 2).

The concerns expressed in this book stem from the use of borders and migration status as a means of exclusion, primarily realised through processes of criminalisa-

S. Pickering, *Women, Borders, and Violence,*
DOI 10.1007/978-1-4419-0271-9_6, © Springer Science+Business Media, LLC 2011

tion or what others have called illegalisation. The specific focus of this book points to the ways in which sex and gender fundamentally shape women's experience of exclusion. It is also a book written with an acute awareness of the position of the academic writer, comfortable in a country replete with some of the most elaborate and far-reaching arrangements that disengage those with certain migration status from the realities of forced migration. Australia, as have other nations, has used unchecked violence against those who move in a current counter to that laid out by its own regulatory arrangements. As a feminist criminologist I remain exercised by the contingencies of gender in processes of crime and justice and in particular the ways in which gender is produced in the social, political and legal relations that shape our attempts at ordering communities, and indeed ordering the globe. I have attempted to approach this study of women as an account of political community that I hope readers will recognise as passing over homogenised accounts of gender and women. In so doing I have sought to destabilise the fixed border, and I hope gone some way to enhancing understanding of the heterogeneity of women's experiences of extra legal border crossings. This book is a modest attempt at thinking differently about borders and extra legal migration by investigating how women have negotiated the unending act of border crossing.

According to the literature, the border is not fixed or immutable, but in constant performance, being constructed and reconstructed in a range of increasingly violent ways. Beginning with women's accounts of extra legal border crossing it is clear there are multiple and shifting meanings of the border. Therefore, it is reasonable to expect that women's experiences of crossing them extra legally are also going to vary and be imbued with a range of meanings that are both context-specific and globally informed. Borders are also increasingly selective and diversified, operating in a range of internal and external locales (Hedetoft, 2003). This book is not a comprehensive account of women's extra legal border crossing. However, it is an overlaid account of how women's experiences of extra legal border crossing point to a range of criminological concerns worthy of further consideration. First and foremost among these is the way in which the border is what Leanne Weber has referred to as "personalised". The experiences of women documented in this book are grounded in a locale but are also informed primarily by their status as non-citizen— a designation that is independent of geographical space. For example, the violence women have experienced is arguably less to do with where they geographically were at the time of their extra legal border crossing and more to do with their non-status (or indeed compromised status) within a society.

Sexual and gender-based violence shaped many of the experiences of the women whose voices are heard in this book. However, the aim here is not to advocate widespread criminalisation in response. Rather, the book examines the processes of forced migration that are the precursors, or the responses, to the sexual violence experienced. To understand sexual violence as experienced by women currently warehoused on Malta, women living in the Thai–Burma borderlands, or women seeking asylum through the courts of the United States, the United Kingdom or Australia requires an understanding of the spaces and processes of violence that irregular migration currently requires. A lack of authorised status, an inability to gain that status in a safe environment and the lack of political clout that goes with that lack of status make possible forms of sexual and gendered violence that overwhelmingly go unchecked. While this book has highlighted the role of a range of non-state actors in the perpetration of this violence, it is important not to overlook that the enactment of border protection regimes and the various arrangements which require forced migrants to travel vast distances consistently either perpetrate or look away from systematic and opportunistic violence. This is not to suggest that the absence of forced migration would absent sexual or gendered violence.

Susan Bumiller has flawlessly argued the case for critically unpacking the alignment of feminist anti-sexual violence campaigns with the drives of neoliberalism. For criminologists the most obvious and dangerous manifestation of this problematic alignment has been the growth in the crime control sector and bureaucratic control over women. However, there remain residual concerns over uncritical approaches to *violence against women* (such as those that view truth as experiential, reduce power to the power of men over women, deny women's agency, preclude men's victimisation, present women as eternal victims and pathologise gender), uncritical approaches within the *gender violence* literature (such as those that see truth as experientially based, reduce power to structural inequalities, accept the omnipotence of violence, reduce gender relations to structural inequality, deny the politics of representation, and lack a focus on the reproduction of difference) (see Shepherd, 2007, for a detailed discussion).

Women's extra legal border crossing is a growing phenomenon. We are limited by the quality and availability of reliable data on women's mobility. There is no reliable scholarly study on global trends in women's extra legal movement, or of the nature and scope of their extra legal border. Extra legal border crossing has been experienced in multifarious ways by women in diverse political, social and legal contexts as detailed in the preceding chapters.

Women fleeing Somalia, a low capacity undemocratic state (Tilly, 2007), experienced a range of state and non-state actor sexual violence which fundamentally shaped their experience of extra legal border crossing. In finally reaching Europe they experienced the violence of refugee warehousing that was the context for the perpetration of both state and non-state harm against them. Malta carries out the unpalatable work of exclusion on behalf of its European neighbours. As Klein has noted, "…if a continent is serious about being a fortress, it also has to invite one or two poor countries within its walls, because somebody has to do the dirty work and heavy lifting" (Klein, 2003). Women's stories from Somalia to Malta suggest extra legal border crossing involves many crossings during periods of exit, transit and reception.

Similarly, women on the Thai–Burma border evidence the ways that the borderland, rather than a border, fundamentally shapes the experience of policing. Extra legal border crossings last lifetimes. Women living and working in the borderland evidence the need to expand narrow conceptions of border policing to consider the complex relationships and policing practices that exert control and facilitate movement in borderlands that are simultaneously a part of and apart from nation-states.

Chapter 4 considered the ways in which law, particularly refugee law, contributes to the repudiation of women's experiences of gender-based violence as a driver of forced migration. A lack of legal status keeps people in a transient state—it keeps them in a legal frontier land, a border region where they are not recognised as equal or deserving and subject to unpredictable consequences. Asylum law requires legally recognisable, chronologically acceptable periods of transit and engagement in the asylum process which the process of fleeing persecution and conflict rarely enables.

Sex trafficking has arguably received the most significant scholarly and policy attention of all matters related to women's extra legal border crossing. Notably, sex trafficking as a transnational crime has seen concern about sex trafficking consume women's legitimate global migration and participation in the sex industry. Sex trafficking has proven highly resistant to border policing efforts and states are increasingly policing out sex trafficking through increased criminalisation and regulatory control over women working in the sex industry.

Collectively, the stories of women considered in the preceding chapters recommend a closer study of borders and their enforcement in terms of transversal spaces, autonomy and exception and permanent transience.

1   Transversal Spaces

Transversality is a way to conceptualise frontier lands, spaces within globalisation and the actors and activities that are empowered by this extra-territorial space. There is a growing body of scholarship that suggests we need to recognise the condition of transversality which does not occupy a space between boundaries, frontiers and borders (sovereign or otherwise) but rather exists "…prior to the conventional sovereign boundaries that enable political inclusions, exclusions and cultural separations across peoples and places" (Soguk & Whitehall, 1999, p. 675). The transversal, Soguk and Whitehall further argue, is defined both for and by migrants and movements. Central to the concept of transversality is the idea that sovereign boundaries/frontiers/borders are temporary and thus constitute an example of transversality itself. Underpinning transversality are a range of processes including border crossing and deterritorialisation (Glissant, 1989). Critiquing the dominant spatial theory upon which much of international relations scholarship depends in discussions of borders and sovereignty, Soguk and Whitehall argue that the concept of transversality does not start with the state as the central agent in life, but with the transversal. Transversality assumes the voices of migrants as a starting point in disrupting state-centric narratives of sovereignty and borders, and the potential of individuals to be alternative legal/political/social subjects in realms where previously they were territorially bounded and silenced. Therefore, applying the concept of transversality does not begin with the languages and accounts of state agents such as border police charged with the policing of transversal spaces. In this regard it could be argued that the policing function itself has developed an investment in transversality as a function of border existence and deterritorialised the policing function from its traditionally territorially grounded role. In as much as the transversal histories of migrants challenge the notion of a sovereign essence, is it possible to imagine a policing function—both central to, but floating apart from, the state—that is able to similarly invest in a border crossing, deterritorialised existence unbounded by temporal or geographic constraint? If so, what does such a transversal policing depend?

Discourses of sovereignty, as an exclusivist form of statehood, may be read as a device for managing the permissible use of force (Pangalangan, 2002)—in this case the deployment of the law enforcement apparatus against asylum seekers. Discourses of sovereignty come to underpin the provision of police protection of a territorial space. As Pangalangan has argued, there has been an (obscured) shift in the "emphasis on the spatial dimension of sovereignty, [which has] disaggregated the competencies bundled up in the erstwhile monolithic concept of sovereignty, allowed new actors to claim these newly spun-off competencies, and recast territorial sovereignty from a source of power to a basis of responsibility" (2002, pp. 164–165). In particular, the (often implicit) changing nature of borders has been a central AFP concern in the deployment of discourses of sovereignty and the integrity of the nation-state. This goes beyond the designation of people smuggling as a form of organised crime that threatens national security and into more general philosophising about the nature and systems of territorially sovereign states.

The borderless function of policing sovereignty requires decreased jurisdictional restraint and increased powers. Unshackled from territorial constraints, this policing push gained momentum just as people smuggling was creating a national moral panic in places such as Australia (Poynting, 2002; Pickering, 2001; Mares, 2001) and just prior to the baton being passed to the terrorist threat in the wake of September 11, 2001. Traditional policing approaches married to territory are unable to deal effectively with these generalised products of globalisation.

McCorquodale has noted that territorial boundaries are not only imaginary but also invented and created by the international legal system: "Boundaries of State territory are the imaginary lines on the surface of the earth which separate the territory of one State from that of another, or from unappropriated territory, or from the Open Sea" (Oppenheim, 1905, cited in McCorquodale, 2001, p. 137). I have attempted to argue that they are also ignored and erased by policing functions that are increasingly transversal.

Transversal policing has been produced by the removal of boundaries between immigration and criminal law, between domestic and transnational policing concerns, and between policing and military functions, as well as between criminal and national security issues. Such policing functions are inherently imprecise—at times almost subterranean. Transversal policing has yielded significant political and material resources for the law enforcement apparatus. Transversal policing is beyond/before nation-states and jurisdictional constraints—free from the territorialising logic of the nation-state and Cartesian dualisms that position policing in opposition to crime and where physical and legislative borders bear down on the nature and scope of policing. The policing of people smuggling cannot be fixed within the spatio-territorial sovereign state, but is always moving and hence itself transforms into a practice of transversality (cf. Soguk & Whitehall, 1999).

The contribution of this book has been to develop the understanding that transversal policing is produced by a range of non-state and criminal actors. Transversal policing, by state and non-state actors, can be understood as a kind of statecraft, a performance of sorts, mostly conducted away from an audience, and not confined to a particular theatre. It is a powerful performance that makes a key contribution to the violent boundary-inscription practices that are meted out as part of border protection policies. At the very moment that it produces a border, however, that border is passed over and the sovereign essence it allegedly protects dissipates. In a similar fashion to the refugee, the policing function moves between and across states, connected to and disconnected from them. However, transversal policing, unlike the transversality of extra legal border crossing, is a powerful condition.

2   Autonomy and Exception

> What happened in the camps so exceeds the juridical concept of crime that the specific juridico-political structure in which those events took place is often simply omitted from consideration. (Agamben, 1998, p. 166)

Women's opportunities to exercise choice in the case studies considered in the preceding chapters are relatively few. To consider autonomy in the context of unchecked violence and conflict in Somalia, or in the law-absent space of refugee warehouses on Malta, is not to glorify or overstate such opportunities, but is to consider both the micro and macro assemblages of decisions and actions that women undertake in conditions in which the law has evaporated. In many ways, forced migration always requires an examination of autonomy and indeed resistance, for it is made up of a matrix of activities that are constitutive of agency. However, it is difficult to reconcile this with the reality of borderlands as spaces which theoreticians from Arendt to Agamben and Bauman regard as devoid of law and humanity.

The person without state protection, Arendt argues, presents as an anomaly for the law and is therefore "at the mercy" of the police. She notes: "…the state, insisting on its sovereign right of expulsion, was forced by the illegal nature of statelessness into admittedly illegal acts" (Arendt, 1968, p. 284). Arendt points to a series of clandestine police practices aimed at smuggling stateless persons out of their jurisdictions and "illegally" into neighbouring countries. Over time, as these practices deteriorated into unedifying inter-state "squabbling" the internment camp filled the need to contain the uncontainable. The internment camp, according to Arendt, became the only "country" the world could offer stateless peoples in the wake of World War II:

> The nation-state, incapable of providing a law for those who had lost the protection of a national government, transferred the whole matter to the police. This was the first time the police in Western Europe had received authority to act on its own, to rule directly over people; in one sphere of public life it was no longer an instrument to carry out and enforce the law, but had become a ruling authority independent of government and ministries. Its

strength and its emancipation from law and government grew in direct proportion to the influx of refugees. (Arendt, 1968, p. 287)

Arendt charts the loss of the political status of refugees, indeed identifies this as a mark of their rightlessness, because of their lack of belonging to a community through which they are legally recognisable: "Their plight is not that they are not equal before the law but that no law exists for them; not that they are oppressed but that nobody wants even to oppress them" (Arendt, 1968, pp. 295–296).

The most fundamental deprivation of human rights, according to Arendt, is the deprivation of a place in the world, which makes "opinions significant and actions effective. Something much more fundamental than freedom and justice, which are rights of citizens, is at stake when belonging to the community into which one is born is no longer a matter of course and not belonging no longer a matter of choice, or when one is placed in a situation where, unless he commits a crime, his treatment by others does not depend on what he does or does not do" (Arendt, 1968, p. 296).

Bauman has observed that: "Hundreds of thousands, sometimes millions of people are chased away from their homes, murdered or forced to run for their lives outside the borders of their country. Perhaps the sole thriving industry in the lands of the latecomers (deviously and often deceitfully dubbed 'developing countries') is the mass production of refugees" (Bauman, p. 33).

The juridically empty space of the "space of exception" (Agamben, 1998) has been repeatedly used to analyse the refugee camp or immigration detention centre. Agamben's account of the camp has been described as indifferent to the question of sex (Asibong, 2009). What the stories in this book indicate is that in the borderlands the "state of exception" radiates out and over borders. Therefore, to focus solely on the border in a state-centric way tells us only so much. We need to also understand the many and various networks that formally and informally either facilitate or prevent mobility which are beyond the state. The ways in which the various borderlands (see Chap. 2) constitute the fertile ground for entrepreneurial activity that may be regarded at any point along a criminal-war-making continuum. Describing the absence of state law in such spaces, Bauman asserts: "The general population of such a state then finds itself in a lawless space; the part of the population that decides to flee the battlefield and manages to escape finds itself in another type of lawlessness, that of the global frontier-land" (Bauman, p. 37).

Agamben argues that there is an important constitutive nexus between the state of exception and the concentration camp which cannot be overestimated (p. 168) because "[t]he camp is the space that is opened when the state of exception begins to become the rule" (Agamben, 1998, pp. 168–169). This creates a space, an excluded space, in which questions around legality or illegality appear to make no sense. For scholars of state crime Agamben identifies the hook:

The correct question to pose concerning the horrors committed in the camps is, therefore, not the hypocritical one of how crimes of such atrocity could be committed against human beings. It would be more honest and, above all, more useful to investigate carefully the juridical procedures and deployments of power by which human beings could be so completely deprived of their rights and prerogatives that no act committed against them could appear any longer as a crime. (1998, p. 171)

Corridors of extra legal exit, transit and entry are being essentially deterritorialised. The transversal denotes a space in which the law is absent or laws are applied only to some populations.

3 Permanent Transience

A key element of transversal spaces, and indeed spaces of exception, is their indeterminate liminality. The condition of permanent transience marks spaces where the journey from conflict to freedom is never complete, and, as the chapters in this book make clear, that are often shaped by ongoing structural and opportunistic violence. Refugee camps, borderlands and endless processes of asylum application evidence this condition of permanent transitoriness. Across the case studies considered in this book permanent transience mark women's experiences of violence and spaces to resist that violence. Women's experiences of being warehoused in Malta, of their ongoing borderland existence on the Thai–Burma border, of their legal and social status through processes of claiming asylum and in the increased criminalisation of their labour within the legitimate sex industry shaped by their precarious relationship with the state. However, being precarious, or transient, had become ongoing, even permanent.

4 Policing a Border

Critical scholars of international relations are responsible for much of the innovation in the reconceptualisation of sovereignty and its relation to the production of the border (see, for example, Devetak, 1995) and understanding borders as borderlands or expanded frontiers. Therefore, it is not surprising that many turn to this field of inquiry to consider the extent to which the border and its enforcement can be reconceived. The work of George Gavrilis is particularly relevant in this regard. Previously, it had been assumed by many in the field of international relations that the enforcement of borders is directly linked to the strength of the state—that is, a weaker state is less secure because its boundaries are porous and unmanageable, stronger states are able to call on effective military and enforcement personnel to uphold the integrity of their borders. Gavrilis' historical and global study of borders offers painstaking detail as to why this assumption is misconceived. He argues that the use of military and law enforcement authorities by strong states often produces counterproductive and perverse effects, while weaker states have opportunities to embrace more pragmatic arrangements. Gavrilis presents this as a paradox: "… states often attempt to micromanage their borders in order to enhance their security, yet the delegation and surrender of authority to boundary administrators ultimately leaves states more secure" (2008, p. 2). As detailed in Chap. 1, there is now a significant body of research which details the ways in which domestic politics inform the performance of border protection, including the political opportunism exercised by political powers. Gavrilis highlights how this has occurred in a range of contexts and notes that especially in African countries states have "inherited vast territories whose borders are perceived as legitimate by the international community but are nonetheless far beyond the coercive reach of their respective authorities" (Gavrilis, 2008, p. 4). If we accept that borders consistently present as sites of violence but are not always violent, then as scholars we need to question how states determine what should and should not be policed along their borders and which institutions should be tasked with these activities. In responding to a similar question, Gavrilis proposes that we look to the decentralised regulation of borders whereby states adopt local arrangements to operate borders in ways that are mutually beneficial for border communities and national interests. He bases his response on an unwavering commitment to the shared character of borders which he sees are constantly reproduced by local conditions, and contends that what is needed is improved institutional design for the operation of borders. "Locally embedded boundary regimes" essentially constitute a bottom-up approach to enforcing borders.

While progressing the debate around productive futures for border control there remains a set of issues that are not resolved by approaches such as that offered by Gavrilis. In short, seeking out more engaged border policing that is better designed and administered requires a more explicit conceptualisation of how borders will be simultaneously more open and more secure (which is often also the aim of such approaches). For example, the work of Benhabib (2004) prompts us to ask of border regimes a justification for their existence, most pertinently in relation to the processes of inclusion and exclusion they enact. In advocating not for open borders, but for porous borders that allow transnational migrations, Benhabib (2004) reminds us of the need for a democratisation of borders whereby those who are subject to the laws enforced at borders have a hand in writing those laws. At the heart of this call is the ongoing concern that states treat citizens and non-citizens differently, which is increasingly problematic for both criminality and justice (Pickering & Weber, 2006).

Extra legal border crossing has been used as evidence of the vulnerability of the states of the Global North. Accounting for the nature of that vulnerability has been notoriously imprecise, yet the generation of easily communicated meaning has been crystal clear: wealthy states of the Global North are vulnerable to difference. This is not to overlook the significant and heinous nature of extremism but to overtly state that what is feared is entirely visible: race, religion, ethnicity and peoples relationship to the production and ownership (or lack thereof) of capital. The Global North overwhelmingly now responds to the most profound loss—that of state protection—with unchecked violence. It responds globally to the locally experienced, globally generated conflicts and state ruptures by attempting to contain the problem locally. Keeping the masses contained has increasingly required their containment near to their countries of origin. Those who are forced to move are primarily and overwhelmingly subjected to violence—social, political and legal violence. This violence is often the absence of action—what Bauman has regarded as disengagement.

The noble journey from persecution to freedom has historically been recorded as a marker of modernisation, as emblematic of the individual and collective vigour and ingenuity upon which entrepreneurial capitalism has thrived. Increasingly, however, this journey is not linear, and nor is it highly regarded. More often than not it is now derided, undermined and constructed as emblematic of the dangerousness of others to the security of the Global North. This book considers the rich and textured accounts of extra legal border crossing in order to understand the gendered consequences of the harm that is perpetrated through processes and spaces which increasingly fall outside the ambit of the law.

Where are the women? This is the question most researchers of forced migration and the enforcement of borders should rightly be asking. When we examine this field of inquiry we find an absence of women, indeed of gender. Curiously or not, this is not to suggest that women are invisible in official narratives of border crossing. For example, women were the focus of the demonising accounts of Australian officials in 2001 who accused female asylum seekers of throwing their children into the water in brinkmanship with the Australian authorities (Marr & Wilkinson, 2003). The ensuing inquiry into the incident found that the women had taken action to save their children's lives and at no time did the attending naval officers think they were sacrificing their children for individual political gain. Women have also been visible in accounts of particular kinds of persecution. In the wake of 9/11 a number of commentators pointed out the hypocrisy of governments in utilising the oppression of women in Afghanistan and indeed Iraq as the rationale for the wars waged by coalition forces (Eisenstein, 2004). The stories of refugee women from those regimes were used to texture the rationales for war-making.

Understanding the ways in which women cross borders extra legally does not necessarily alter the fundamentals of the various critiques of the construction of borderlands and the disengagement of the populace and the state from what happens within, around and en route to borderlands. However, focusing on women's accounts yields insight into how gender-based violence, gendered social mores and compromised transnational networks are shaped in nature and form by the criminalisation and punishment of those crossing borders extra legally. In responses to perceived threats of transnational organised crime, Beare (2003) has argued, we are witnessing a hijacking of criminal justice to meet political and strategic ends. The border has been a key site for this with a range of implications for women.

As Eisenstein remarked on her task in considering relations of power, especially post 9/11, "[m]y purpose is to move towards a more inclusive viewing of humanity by looking for absences, listening for silences, and imagining beyond my own limits" (2004, p. xv). This book is an attempt to understand women's extra legal mobility in the context in which it occurs generated by listening to the voices and the silences to make sense of the ways borders and violence impact on women.

If sovereignty is performative, and the enforcement of borders constitutive of this performance, and if gender is performative, then the key concern of this book has been the nature, scope and impact of the violence that is woven through sovereign and gender performances. The focus on extra legal border crossing is a call for international criminological attention to the violence that is marshalled by states to protect their borders, as well as the violence enacted by non-state actors in the ripples emanating out from fortified borders.

5   Summary

Borders are of increasing significance to social science for both their coercive and ideological force. The noble journey from persecution to freedom has historically been recorded as a marker of modernisation, as emblematic of the individual and collective vigour and ingenuity upon which entrepreneurial capitalism has thrived. Increasingly, however, this journey is not linear, and nor is it highly regarded. More often than not it is now derided, undermined and constructed as emblematic of the dangerousness of others for the security of the Global North. This book considers the rich and textured accounts of extra legal border crossing in order to understand the gendered consequences of the harm that is perpetrated through processes and spaces which increasingly fall outside the ambit of the law. This chapter considers the evidence presented in the book in light of increasingly transversal policing practices, states of exception and permanent transience.

Bibliography

Agamben, G. (1998). *Homo sacer: Sovereign, power and bare life* (trans: D. Heller-Roazen). Stanford: Stanford University Press.

Agamben, G. (2005). *States of exception* (trans: K. Attell). Chicago: Chicago University Press.

Alcorn, G., & Minchin, L. (2003, October 25). A red light on trafficking. *The Age, Insight.*

Amnesty International. (2007). Denied refuge: The effect of the closure of the Kenya/Somali border on thousands of Somali asylum-seekers and refugees (May 2, 2007; pp. 3–4). http://www.amnesty.org/en/library/info/AFR32/002/2007. Accessed 14 Jan 2009.

Amore, K. (2007). Malta. In A. Triandafyllidou & R. Gropas (Eds.), *European immigration: A sourcebook* (pp. 237–248). Hampshire: Ashgate.

ANAO (2009). *Management of the Australian Government's Action Plan to Eradicate Trafficking in Persons*, Report No. 30, Canberra, Australian National Audit Office.

Anker, D. (2002). Refugee law, gender, and the human rights paradigm. *Harvard Human Rights Journal, 15*, 133–154.

Anti-People Trafficking Interdepartmental Commission. (APTIC) (2009). Trafficking in persons: The Australian government response, January 2004–April 2009. Commonwealth of Australia Canberra: Attorney-General's Department. http://www.ag.gov.au/www/agd/rwpattach.nsf/VAP/(084A3429FD57AC0744737F8EA134BACB)~IDC±Annual±Report_WEB.pdf/$file/IDC±Annual±Report_WEB.pdf.

Arboleda, E., & Hoy, I. (1993). The convention refugee definition in the west: Disharmony of interpretation and application. *International Journal of Refugee Law, 5*(1), 66–90.

Arendt, H. (1968). *The origins of totalitarianism*. Orlando: Harcourt.

Asibong, A. (2009). Femina sacra: The 'war on/of terror', women and the feminine. *Security Dialogue, 40*, 29–49.

ASS. (2008). *Population/people*. National Regional Profile: Australia.

Attorney-General's Department. (2003). Australian government announces major package to combat people trafficking. Media Release (R002/003). http://www.ag.gov.au/www/Minister-RuddockHome.nsf/Web±Pages/562B49E37E59755FCA256DBE001218B9?OpenDocument. Accessed 13 Oct 2003.

Attorney-General's Department. (2007). More resources to combat people trafficking. Media Release (Budget 2007–08). http://www.ag.gov.au/www/agd/agd.nsf/Page/RWP7561D03F6952F-B64CA2572D4000BB873. Accessed 8 May 2007.

AusAID. (2003). Minister for Foreign Affairs: Australian initiative to combat people trafficking. Media Release (AA 03 034). http://www.ausaid.gov.au/media/previous.cfm. Accessed 19 June 2003.

Australian Bureau of Statistics (ABS). (2007). Census of population and housing—Australia: Ancestry (Full Classification List) by Sex. A. B. o. Statistics. Canberra: Australian Bureau of Statistics. Cat No 2068.0: 2006 Census Tables.

S. Pickering, *Women, Borders, and Violence,*
DOI 10.1007/978-1-4419-0271-9, © Springer Science+Business Media, LLC 2011

Ayet P. J. (2008). *Report on the evaluation and future development of FRONTEX Agency: Statistical data*. Commission of the European Communities, SEC (2008) 150, Brussels.

Bacon, D. (2007). *Illegal people: How globalization creates migration and criminalizes immigrants*. Boston: Beacon Press.

Bahrampour, T. (2009, October 1). Clearer rules urged for asylum seekers. *The Washington Post*.

Banerjee, P. (2010). *Borders, histories, existences: Gender and beyond*. New Delhi: Sage Publications.

Barsky, R. (1994). *Constructing a productive other: Discourse theory and the convention refugee hearing*. Amsterdam: John Benjamins Publishing.

Bartolomei, L., Pittaway, E., & Pittaway, E. (2003). Who am I? Identity and citizenship in Kakuma refugee camp in northern Kenya. *Development, 46*(3), 87–93.

Bauman, Z. (2007). *Liquid times: Living in an age of uncertainty*. Cambridge: Polity Press.

Beare, M. (Ed.). (2003). *Critical reflections on transnational organized crime, money laundering and corruption*. Toronto: University of Toronto Press.

Benhabib, S. (2004). *The rights of others: Aliens, residents and citizens*. Cambridge: Cambridge University Press.

Besteman, C. (2006). Representing violence and 'othering' in Somalia. *Cultural Anthropology, 11*(1), 120–133.

Bradbury, M., Menkhaus, K., & Marchal, R. (2001). *Human development report Somalia, 2001*. New York: United Nations Development Program.

Britannica, E. (2009). Malta. Encyclopaedia Britannica Online.

British Broadcasting Corporation (BBC). (2009). Overview of Burma sanctions. http://news.bbc.co.uk/2/hi/asia-pacific/8195956.stm.

Bumiller, K. (2008). *In an abusive state: How neoliberalism appropriated the feminist movement against sexual violence*. London: Duke University Press.

Burmese Women's Union (BWU). (2007). Caught between two hells. www.womenofburma.org/Report/Caught%20between%20two%20hells.pdf.

Burn, J., & Simmons, F. (2005). Rewarding witnesses, ignoring victims: An evaluation of the new trafficking visa framework. *Immigration Review, 24*, 6–13.

Burn, J., Blay, S., & Simmons, F. (2005). Combating human trafficking: Australia's response to modern day slavery. *Australian Law Journal, 79*(9), 543–552.

Burn, J., Simmons, F., & Costello, G. (2006). *Australian NGO shadow report on trafficked women in Australia*. Submitted to the 34th session of the Committee for the Convention on the Elimination of All Forms of Discrimination Against Women. New York: UNANIMA International Congregation of Sisters of the Good Shepherd.

Bustamante, J. (2006). *Report of the special rapporteur on human rights of migrants: Specific groups and individual migrant workers*. C. o. H. Rights. New York: Economic and Social Council.

Calavita, K. (2003). A reserve army of delinquents, punishment and society: The criminalisation and economic punishment of immigrants in Spain. *Punishment and Society, 5*(4), 399–413.

Calavita, K. (2008). Deflecting the immigration debate: Globalization, immigrant agency, 'strange bedfellows' and beyond. *Contemporary Sociology, 37*(4), 302–305.

Carpenter, J. (2006). The gender of control. In S. Pickering & L. Weber (Eds.), *Borders, mobility and technologies of control* (pp. 167–177). New York: Springer.

Carrington, K., & Hearn, J. (2003). Trafficking and the sex industry: From impunity to protection. *Current Issue Brief*, (28), 2002–03, Canberra: Australian Parliamentary Library. http://www.aph.gov.au/library/pubs/CIB/2002-03/03cib28.pdf.

Caruana, R. C. (2007). The accession of Malta to the EU. In G. Vassiliou (Ed.), *The accession story: The EU from fifteen to twenty-five countries* (pp. 259–296). Oxford: Oxford University Press.

Centre for Peace and Conflict Studies (CPCS). (2008). Listening to voices from inside: Myanmar civil society's response to Cyclone Nargis. Centre for Peace and Conflict Studies, Phnom Penh. http://www.relief.web.int/rw/rwb/nsf/db900sid/SNAA-7RR92S?OpenDocument. Accessed 22 Jan 2010.

Charlesworth, H., & Chinkin, C. (2000). *The boundaries of international law*. Manchester: Manchester University Press.

Chaudhry, M. (2007). Particular social groups post Fornah. *Journal of Immigration, Asylum and Nationality Law, 21*(2), 137–146.

Chuang, J. (2006). The United States as global sheriff: Using unilateral sanctions to combat human trafficking. *Michigan Journal of International Law, 27*, 437–494.

Coffman, J. (2007). Producing FGM in US courts: Political asylum in the post-Kasinga era. *Africa Today, 53*(4), 59–84.

Cohen, S. (2001). *States of denial: Knowing about atrocities and suffering*. Malden: Polity Press.

Cole, D. (2008). *Enemy aliens*. New York: The New Press.

Committee on Civil Liberties, Justice and Home Affairs (LIBE). (2006). *Report by the committee on civil Liberties, Justice and Home Affairs (LIBE) delegation on its visit to the administrative detention centres in Malta*. Brussels: LIBE.

Conklin, W. (1997). The assimilation of the other within a master discourse. In H. Riggins (Ed.), *The language and politics of exclusion: Others in discourse*. Sage: Thousand Oaks.

Coomaraswamy, R. (2003). Fishing in the stream of migration: Modern forms of trafficking and women's freedom of movement. In International Association of Refugee Law Judges, 5th Conference, Wellington, New Zealand, p. 22.

Correa-Velez, I., & Gifford, S. M. (2007). When the right to be counted doesn't count: The politics and challenges of researching the health of asylum seekers. *Critical Public Health, 17*(3), 273–281.

Crawley, H. (2001). *Refugees and gender: Law and process*. London: Jordan.

Crisp, J. (1999). No solution in sight: The problem of protracted refugee situations in Africa. *Refugee Survey Quarterly, 22*(4), 114–150.

Crisp, J. (2000). A state of insecurity: The political economy of violence in Kenya's refugee camps. *African Affairs, 99*, 601–632.

Crisp, J. (2003). Why do we know so little about refugees? *Forced Migration Review, 18*, 55.

Crisp, J. (2004). Refugees and the politics of asylum. *The Political Quarterly, 74*(1), 75–87.

Dauvergne, C. (2008). *Making people illegal*. Cambridge: Cambridge University Press.

Department of Information (DOI). (2009). The Maltese Islands. http://www.doi.gov.mt/EN/islands/location.asp. Accessed 17 Sept 2009.

Development of the Frontex Agency, Statistical Data, SEC. (2008). 150. Brussels, Commission on the Commission of the European Communities.

Devetak, R. (1995). Incomplete states: Theories and practices of statecraft. In J. Macmillan & A. Linklater (Eds.), *Boundaries in Question*. London: Pinter Publishers.

Ditmore, M., & Wijers, M. (2003). *Sex, money, migration and crime. The negotiations on the United Nations Protocol on Trafficking in Persons*. Utrecht: Nemesis.

Donnan, H., & Wilson, T. (1999). *Borders: Frontiers of identity, nation and state*. Oxford: Berg Publishers.

Doty, R. (1996). Sovereignty and the nation: Constructing the boundaries of national identity. In T. Biersteker & C. Weber (Eds.), *State sovereignty as social construct*. Cambridge: Cambridge University Press.

Edelman, M. (1988). *Constructing the political spectacle*. Chicago: University of Chicago Press.

Editorial. (2009, November 9). Rody Alvarado's odyssey. *The New York Times*.

Edwards, S. (2007). Female genital mutilation: Violence against girls and women as a particular social group: Fornah v Secretary of State for the Home Department. *The Denning Law Journal, 19*, 271–278.

Eisenstein, Z. (2004). *Against empire: Feminisms, racism and the west*. Melbourne: Spinifex Press.

Eschbach, K. (1999). Death at the border. *International Migration Review, 33*.

European Commission against Racism and Intolerance (ECRI). (2008). *Third report on Malta*. Strasbourg: Council of Europe.

Eurostat. (2008a). *Europe in figures: Eurostat Yearbook 2008*. Luxembourg: European Communities.

Eurostat. (2008b). *Key figures on Europe 2007/2008 edition.* General and Regional Statistics. G. Schäfer. Luxembourg: Statistical Office of the European Communities.

Fairclough, N. (1998). Political discourse in the media: An analytical framework. In A. Bell & P. Garrett (Eds.), *Approaches to media discourse* (pp. 142–162). Oxford: Blackwell.

Falcon, S. (2001). Rape as a weapon of war: Advancing human rights for women at the US-Mexico border. *Social Justice, 28*(2), 31–51.

Fawkes, J. (2003). Parliamentary Joint Committee on the Australian Crime Commission: Inquiry into trafficking in women for sexual servitude: Submission No 27, for Scarlet Alliance, September 29, 2003. http://www.aph.gov.au/Senate/committee/acc_ctte/sexual_servitude/submissions/sublist.htm.

Finnane, M. (2009). Controlling 'aliens': Origins and politics of a policing role in Australia. *Policing and Society, 19*(4), 442–467.

Fitzgerald, M. (1998). Firewood, violence against women, and hard choices in Kenya. *Refugees International,* http://www.refintl.org/.

Ford, M. (2001). Sex slaves and loopholes: Exploring the legal framework and federal responses to the trafficking of Thai 'contract girls' for sexual exploitation to Melbourne, Australia. Fitzroy: Project Respect. http://www.projectrespect.org.au/. Accessed 15 March 2004.

Frydman, L., & Seelinger, K. (2008, September 1). Kasinga's protection undermined? Recent developments in female genital cutting jurisprudence. *Bender's Immigration Journal, 13,* 1073–1105.

Gardner, D. (2004, March 11). Cotler wrong to let US define sex-trade issue: Complex problem— global trafficking of prostitutes is more than a good vs evil issue. *The Gazette (editorial).* Montreal, Quebec.

Gardner, J., & El Bushra J. (Eds.). (2004). *Somalia: The untold story, the war through the eyes of Somali women.* London: Pluto Press Publishing.

Gavrilis, G. (2008). *The dynamics of interstate boundaries.* Cambridge: Cambridge University Press.

Glissant, E. (1989). *Caribbean discourse.* Charlottesville: University Press of Virginia.

Goodey, J. (2003). Migration, crime and victimhood: Responses to sex trafficking in the EU. *Punishment & Society, 5*(4), 415–431.

Goodey, J. (2004). Sex trafficking in women from Central and East European countries: Promoting a 'victim-centred' and 'woman-centred' approach to criminal justice intervention. *Feminist Review, 76,* 26–45.

Gready, P. (2004). Conceptualising globalisation and human rights: Boomerangs and borders. *International Journal of Human Rights, 8,* 345–354.

Greatbatch, J. (1989). The gender difference: Feminist critiques of refugee discourse. *International Journal of Refugee Law, 1*(4), 518–527.

Green, P. (2006). State crime beyond borders. In S. Pickering & L. Weber (Eds.), *Borders, mobility and technologies of control.* New York: Springer.

Green, P., & Grewcock, M. (2002). The war against illegal immigration: State crime and the construction of a European identity. *Current Issues in Criminal Justice, 14*(1), 87–101.

Green, P., & Ward, T. (2009). The transformation of violence in Iraq. *The British Journal of Criminology, 49,* 609–627.

Grewcock, M. (2010). *Border crimes: Australia's war against illicit migration.* Sydney: Institute of Criminology.

Hagmann, T. (2005). From state collapse to duty free shop: Somalia's path to modernity. *African Affairs, 104*(416), 525–535.

Harrell-Bond B., Voutira, E., & Leopold, M. (1992). Counting the refugees: Gifts, givers, patrons and clients. *Journal of Refugee Studies, 5*(3/4), 205–225.

Harris, L. (2009, July 21). Give me your tired, your poor, your battered: How does asylum for abused women actually work? http://www.salon.com/life/broadsheet/feature/2009/07/21/asylum_for_domestic_violence/index.html.

Hathaway, J. (1991). *The law of refugee status.* Toronto: Butterworths.

Hathaway, J. (2003). What's in a label? *European Journal of Migration and Law, 5*(1), 1–21.

Hathaway, J. (2008). The human rights quagmire of 'human trafficking'. *Virginia Journal of International Law, 49*(1), 1–59.

Hedetoft, U. (2003). *The global turn: National encounters with the world.* Aalborg: Aalborg University Press.

House of Representatives, Migration Amendment (Complementary Protection) Bill 2009, Second Reading Speech, Wednesday 9 September 2009.

Howitt, R. (2001). Frontiers, borders, edges: Liminal challenges to the hegemony of exclusion. *Australian Geographical Studies, 39*, 233–245.

Human Rights Watch (HRW). (1993). *Seeking refuge, finding terror: The widespread rape of Somali women refugees in north eastern Kenya.* New York: HRW.

Human Rights Watch (HRW). (2008). *'So much to fear': War crimes and the devastation of Somalia.* New York: HRW.

Human Rights Watch (HRW). (2009a). *Pushed back, pushed around: Italy's forced return of boat migrants and asylum seekers, Libya's mistreatment of migrants and asylum seekers.* http://www.hrw.org/en/node/85582/section/14.

Human Rights Watch (HRW). (2009b). *From horror to hopelessness: Kenya's forgotten Somali refugee crisis.* New York: HRW.

Human Rights Watch (HRW). (2009c). *Hostile shores: Abuse and refoulement of asylum seekers and refugees in Yemen.* New York: HRW.

Hunter, C. (2002). Khawar and Migration Legislation Amendment Bill (No 6) 2001: Why narrowing the definition of a refugee discriminates against gender-related claims. *Australian Journal of Human Rights, 8*(1), 107–120.

ICG. (2008). Burma/Myanmar after Nargis: Time to normalise aid relations. *Asia Report* No. 161, 20 October 2008.

ICG. (2009). Myanmar: Towards the Elections International Crisis Group. *Asia Report* No. 174, 20 August 2009.

Illegal Immigration Reform and Immigrant Responsibility Act. (1996).

Indra, D. (1987). Gender: A key dimension in the refugee experience. *Refuge, 6*(3).

Indra, D. (Ed.). (1999). *Engendering forced migration.* Oxford: Berghahn Books.

International Commission of Jurists (ICJ). (2008). *Malta: ICJ Submission to the UN Univeral Periodic Review.* Geneva: International Commission of Jurists.

Iselin, B. (2003). Parliamentary Joint Committee on the Australian Crime Commission—Inquiry into trafficking in women for sexual servitude: Submission No. 6 (for Iselin Consulting). 11 September 2003. http://www.aph.gov.au/Senate/committee/acc_ctte/sexual_servitude/submissions/sublist.htm. Accessed 22 March 2004.

Jesuit Refugee Service (JRS). (2006). *Asylum in Malta: What you should know: Guide to the asylum procedure for immigrants in detention.* Valetta: Jesuit Refugee Service.

Joint Committee on the Australian Crime Commission (JCACC). (2003). Proof Committee Hansard: Trafficking in women for sexual servitude. Melbourne 18 November 2003. http://www.aph.gov.au/Senate/committee/acc_ctte/sexual_servitude/index.htm.

Joint Committee on the Australian Crime Commission (JCACC). (2004a). Proof Committee Hansard: Trafficking in women for sexual servitude. Sydney 25 February 2004. http://www.aph.gov.au/Senate/committee/acc_ctte/sexual_servitude/index.htm.

Joint Committee on the Australian Crime Commission (JCACC). (2004b). Proof Committee Hansard: Trafficking in women for sexual servitude. Canberra 26 February 2004. http://www.aph.gov.au/Senate/committee/acc_ctte/sexual_servitude/index.htm.

Joint Committee on the Australian Crime Commission (JCACC). (2004c). Proof Committee Hansard: Trafficking in women for sexual servitude. Canberra 30 February 2004. http://www.aph.gov.au/Senate/committee/acc_ctte/sexual_servitude/index.htm.

Jupp, J. (2001). *The Australian people: An encyclopedia of the nation, its people and their origins.* Cambridge: Cambridge University Press.

Kapur, R. (2002). Un-veiling women's rights in the 'war on terrorism'. *Duke Journal of Gender Law and Policy, 9*, 210–225.

Kapur, R. (2005). *Erotic justice, postcolonialism. Subject and rights.* London: Glasshouse Press.

Karlsen, E. (2009a). Migration Amendment (Complementary Protection) Bill 2009. Bills Digest. Canberra: Parliament of Australia.

Karlsen, E. (2009b). *Complementary protection for asylum seekers: Overview of the international and Australian legal frameworks*. Research Paper. Canberra: Parliament of Australia.

Kelly, E. (2002). *Journeys of jeopardy: A commentary on current research on trafficking of women and children for sexual exploitation within Europe*. London: International Organisation for Migration.

Kittiwongsakul, P. (2009). Thailand starts deporting Hmong to Laos, *The Age*, December 28.

Klein, N. (2003, 16 January). Fortress continents. *The Guardian*, p. 23.

Koser, K., & Pinkerton, C. (2002). The social networks of asylum seekers and the dissemination of information about countries of asylum. *Home Office Findings No. 165*. London: Home Office.

Kramer, T. (2009). Neither war nor peace: The future of the cease-fire agreements in Burma. Amsterdam: Transnational Institute. http://www.tni.org/report/neither-war-nor-peace). Accessed 10 Jan 2010.

Kretsedemas, P., & Brotherton, D. (Eds.). (2008). *Keeping out the other: A critical introduction to immigration enforcement today*. New York: Columbia University Press.

Kyle, D., & Koslowski, R. (2001). *Global human smuggling: Comparative perspectives*. Baltimore: John Hopkins University Press.

Lambert, C., Pickering, S., & Adler, C. (2003). *Critical chatter: Women and human rights in South East Asia*. Durham: Carolina Academic Press.

Lamont, L. (2003, March 13). Sold at 12: Nightmare ends in death. *Sydney Morning Herald*, p. 7.

Lawyers Committee for Human Rights. (2002). *Refugee women at risk*. New York: Lawyers Committee for Human Rights.

Lewis, A. (1996, April 19). Abroad at home: Slamming the door. *The New York Times*.

Lewis, I. M. (2002). *A modern history of Somalia: Nation and state in the horn of Africa* (4th ed.). Oxford: James Curry.

LIBE (2006). Report by the committee on civil liberties, justice and home affairs (LIBE) delegation on it's visit to the detention centres in Malta. Committee on Civil Liberties, Justice and Home Affairs, 30 March 2006, Brussels.

Lindley, A. (2009). Crisis and displacement in Somalia. *Forced Migration Review, 33*, 18–19.

Luibheid, E. (2002). *Entry denied: Controlling sexuality at the border*. Minneapolis: University of Minnesota Press.

Luibheid, E. (2005). Introduction: Queering migration and citizenship. In E. Luibheid & L. Cantu (Eds.), *Queer migrations: Sexuality, US citizenship and border crossings* (pp. ix–xlvi). Minneapolis: University of Minnesota Press.

Lutterbeck, D. (2009). Small frontier island: Malta and the challenge of irregular immigration. *Mediterranean Quarterly,* (Winter), 119–144.

MacLeod, A. (1995). Hegemonic relations and gender resistance: The new veiling as accommodating protest in Cairo. In B. Laslett, J. Brenner & Y. Arat (Eds.), *Rethinking the political: Gender, resistance and the state*. Chicago: Chicago University Press.

Maddigan, J. (2010). Inquiry into trafficking for sex work. Final report (Committee on the Prevention of Drugs and Crime). Melbourne: Victorian State Government.

Makkai, T. (2003). *Thematic discussion on trafficking in human beings: Report from the workshop in human beings, especially women and children*. Canberra: Australian institute of Criminology. http://www.aic.gov.au/conferences/other/makkai_toni/2003-05-traffick.pdf.

Maltzahn, K. (2003). Parliamentary Joint Committee on the Australian Crime Commission: Inquiry into trafficking in women for sexual servitude: Submission No. 25 (for Project Respect). 29 September 2003. http://www.aph.gov.au/Senate/committee/acc_ctte/sexual_servitude/submissions/sublist.htm. Accessed 22 March 2004.

Maltzahn, K. (2004). Paying for servitude: Trafficking in women for prostitution. Pamela Denoon Lecture 2004. http://www.wel.org.au/announce/denoon/04lecture.htm.

Mares, P. (2001). *Borderline*. Sydney: UNSW Press.

Marr, D., & Wilkinson, M. (2003). *Dark victory*. Sydney: Allen & Unwin.

Masurelle, V., & Poykko, J. (2007). *Report of Exchange Programme in Malta*. Fedasil: European Network of Asylum Reception Organisations.

Mathew, P. (2000). Conformity or persecution: China's one child policy and refugee status. *UNSW Law Review, 23*, 103–134.

McAdam, J. (2005). *Complementary protection and beyond: How states deal with human rights protection. New issues in refugee research*. Working Paper No. 118. UNHCR: Geneva.

McCorquodale, R. (2001). International law, boundaries and imagination. In D. Miller & S. Hashmi (Eds.), *Boundaries and justice: Diverse ethical perspectives*. Princeton: Princeton University Press.

McCulloch, J., & Pickering, S. (2009). The violence of refugee incarceration. In J. McCulloch & P. Scraton (Eds.), *The violence of incarceration* (pp. 225–243). London: Routledge.

McSherry, B. (2007). Trafficking in persons: A critical analysis of the new criminal code offences. *Current Issues in Criminal Justice, 18*(3), 385–398.

Melossi, D. (2003). 'In a peaceful life': Migration and the crime of modernity in Europe/Italy. *Punishment and Society, 5*(4), 371–398.

Menkhaus, K. (2004). *Somalia: State collapse and the threat of terrorism* (Adelphi paper No. 364). Oxford: Oxford University Press.

Michalowski, R. (2007). Border militarization and migrant suffering: A case of transnational social injury. *Social Justice, 31*(5).

Milivojević, S., & Pickering, S. (2008). Football and sex: The 2006 FIFA world cup and sex trafficking. *Temida, 11*(2), 21–47.

Minchin, L. (2003, October 21). Australia's sex slavery trade thriving: Expert. *The Age*, p. 3.

Minister for Immigration and Multicultural and Indigenous Affairs. (2003). Stopping people trafficking in sex industry a high priority. Media Release 1 April 2003 MPS 20/2003. http://www.minister.immi.gov.au/media_releases/ruddock_media03/r03020.htm.

Minister for Justice and Customs. (2003a). Transcript of doorstop. 13 October 2003. http://www.ag.gov.au/www/justiceministerHome.nsf/Web±Pages/0AED0AF57363AADBCA256DBE007AB4AE?OpenDocument.

Minister for Justice and Customs. (2003b). Commonwealth tightens screws on people traffickers. Media Release 18 December 2003 E189/0. http://www.ag.gov.au/www/justiceministerHome.nsf/Web±Pages/A9872CABA7783EADCA256E01000D0750?OpenDocument.

Ministry for Justice and Home Affairs (MJHA). (2009). *Setup: The office of the refugee commissioner*. Valetta: MJHA.

MJHA and Ministry for the Family and Social Solidarity (MFSS). (2005). *Irregular immigrants, refugees and integration: Policy document*. Valetta: MJHA/MFSS.

Musalo, K. (2008). *Annual Report*. Hastings: Center for Gender and Refugee Studies, University of California.

Musse, F. (2004). War crimes against women and girls. In J. Gardner & J. El Bushra (Eds.), *Somalia: The untold story, the war through the eyes of Somali women*. London: Pluto Press Publishing.

National Statistics Office (NSO). (2009). *World Refugee Day: 2009*. Valetta: NSO.

Nevins, J. (2002). Operation gatekeeper: The rise of the 'illegal alien' and the making of the US–Mexico boundary. New York: Routledge.

Noor, H. (2007). Emergency within an emergency: Somali IDPs. *Forced Migration Review, 28*, 29–31.

Norberry, J., & Guest, K. (1999). Bills Digest No.167 1998-99L: Criminal Code Amendment (Slavery and Sexual Servitude) Bill 1999. Canberra: Australian Parliamentary Library. http://www.aph.gov.au/library/pubs/bd/1998-99/99bd167.htm. Accessed 5 April 2004.

O'Brien, N., & Wynhausen, E. (2003, September 27). Officials 'hound' sex slave informers. *The Weekend Australian*, p. 7.

Ortiz, V. (2001). The unbearable ambiguity of the border. *Social Justice, 28*(2), 96–112.

Ostergaard, M. (2008). *Europe's 'boat people': Mixed migration flows by sea into southern Europe*. Report of the Rapporteur to the Committee on Migration, Refugees, and Population. Belgium: Parliamentary Assembly, Council of Europe.

Pangalangan, R. (2002). Territorial sovereignty: Command title and expanding claims of the commons. In D. Miller & S. Hashmi (Eds.), *Boundaries and justice: Diverse ethical perspectives* (pp. 164–182). Princeton: Princeton University Press.

Pearson, E. (2007). 'Australia' in Global Alliance Against Trafficking in Women (GAATW). In Global Alliance Against Traffic in Women (Ed.), *Collateral damage: The impact of anti-trafficking measures on human rights around the world* (pp. 28–60). Bangkok: GAATW.

Pether, P., & Threadgold, T. (2000). Feminist methodologies in discourse analysis: Sex, property, equity. In C. Poynton & T. Threadgold (Eds.), *Culture and Text*. Sydney: Allen and Unwin.

Pickering, S. (2001). Common sense and original deviancy: News discourses and asylum seekers in Australia. *Journal of Refugee Studies, 14*, 169–186.

Pickering, S. (2004). The production of sovereignty and the rise of transversal policing: People smuggling and federal policing. *Australian and New Zealand Journal of Criminology, 37*(3), 340–358.

Pickering, S. (2005). *Refugees and state crime*. Sydney: Federation Press.

Pickering, S., & Weber, L. (2006). *Borders, mobility and technologies of control*. New York: Springer.

Pittaway, E., & Bartolomei, L. (2004). *Field research report. Kakuma, Kenya and Thai–Burma Border*. Sydney: Centre for Refugee Research, University of New South Wales.

Plantenga, J., Remery, C., Figueiredo, H., & Smith, M. (2009). Towards a European Union gender equality index. *Journal of European Social Policy, 19*(1), 19.

Pollard, J. (2003). Girl wasn't sold as a sex slave revealed: The tragedy that shocked Sydney was a lie. *The Daily Telegraph*, p. 5.

Poynting, S. (2002). Bin Laden in the suburbs: Attacks on Arab Muslim Australians before and after September 11, *Current Issues in Criminal Justice, 14*(2).

Preston, J. (2009, October 30). US may be open to asylum for spouse abuse. *The New York Times*.

Rackley, E. (2008). What a difference difference makes: Gendered harms and judicial diversity. *International Journal of the Legal Profession, 15*(1–2), March–July 2008, 37–56.

Raymond, J. (2002). The new UN trafficking protocol. *Women's Studies International Forum, 25*(5), 491–502.

Reus-Smit, C. (2001). Human rights and the social construction of sovereignty. *Review of International Studies, 27*, 519–538.

Roxon, N., Maltzahn, K., & Costello, G. (2004). *'One victim of trafficking is one too many': Counting the human cost of trafficking*. Collingwood: Project Respect.

Ruddock, P. (2002). Offshore processing developments and related savings. www.minister.immi.gov.au/media_releases/media02/r02033.htm. Accessed 5 Sept 2002.

Rushdie, S. (2002). *Step across this line: Selected non-fiction 1992–2002*. London: Cape.

Sassen, S. (1998). *Globalization and its discontents: Essays on the new mobility of people and money*. New York: The New Press.

Sassen, S. (1999), *Guests and Aliens*. New York: The New Press.

Sassen, S. (2000). Women's burden: Counter-geographies of globalization and the feminization of survival. *Journal of International Affairs, 53*(2), 504–524.

Sassen, S. (2002). Women's burden: Counter-geographies of globalization and the feminization of survival. *Nordic Journal of International Law, 71*(2), 255–274.

Saunders, P., & Soderlund, G. (2003). Traveling threats: Trafficking as discourse. *Canadian Woman Studies, 22*, 35–46.

Scicluna, S., & Knepper, P. (2008). The British Empire and imprisonment in Malta in the early nineteenth century. *British Journal of Criminology, 48*, 502–521.

Segrave, M. (2008). Trafficking in persons as labour exploitation, *Proceedings of the 2nd Australian Critical Criminology Conference*. In C. Cunneen & M. Salter (Eds.), Sydney: Crime and Justice Research Network.

Segrave, M. (2009). Human trafficking and human rights, *Australian Journal of Human Rights, 14*(2), 71–94.

Segrave, M., & Milivojevic, S. (2005). Sex trafficking: A new agenda. *Social Alternatives, 24*,(2), 11–16.

Segrave, M., & Milivojevic, S. (2010). Auditing the Australian response to trafficking. *Current Issues in Criminal Justice, 22*(1), 63–80.

Segrave, M., Milivojevic, S., & Pickering, S. (2009). *Sex trafficking: International context & response*. Devon: Willan Publishing.

Senate Legal & Constitutional Affairs Committee Hansard. (2002). Senate Estimates Hearing: Immigration and Multicultural & Indigenous Affairs. 11 February 2003. http://www.aph.gov.au/hansard/senate/commttee/s6144.pdf.

Shacknove, A. (1985). Who is a Refugee? *Ethics, 95*(2), 274–284.

Shepherd, L. (2007). *Gender, violence and security*. London: Zed Books.

Sinha, A. (2001). Domestic violence and US asylum law: Eliminating the 'cultural hook' for claims involving gender-related persecution. *New York University Law Review, 76*, 1562–1598.

Soguk, N. (1999). *States and strangers: Refugees and displacements of statecraft*. Minneapolis: University of Minnesota Press.

Soguk, N., & Whitehall, G. (1999). Wandering grounds: Transversality, identity, territoriality, and movement. *Millennium: Journal of International Studies, 28*, 675–698.

Soler, E., & Musalo, K. (July 18, 2009). Time to end an asylum limbo for abused women. *The Washington Post*.

Spijkerboer, T. (1994). *Women and refugee law: Beyond the public/private domain*. The Hague: The Emancipation Council.

The Law Report. (2003). Trafficking women for prostitution. ABC Radio National broadcast 28 October 2003. http://www.abc.net.au/rn/talks/8.30/lawrpt/stories/s975557.htm.

Tilly, C. (1995). War making and state making as organized crime. In P. Evans, D. Rueschemeyer, & T. Skocpol (Eds.), *Bringing the state back in*. Cambridge: Cambridge University Press.

Tilly, C. (2003). *The politics of collective violence*, Cambridge: Cambridge University Press.

Tilly, C. (2007). *Democracy*. Cambridge: Cambridge University Press.

Tripartite Core Group (TCG). (2008). Post Nargis Joint Assessment July 2008. www.aseansec.org.

Turner, S. (1999). *Angry young men in camps: Gender, age and class relations among Burundian refugees in Tanzania*, New Issues in Refugee Research Working Paper No. 9.

UN Human Rights Council (HRC). (2009). *Working group on the Universal Periodic Review: Malta*. Geneva: General Assembly United Nations.

UN Working Group on Arbitrary Detention (WAGD). (2009). *Annex to the press release on the visit of the United Nations Working Group on Arbitrary Detention to Malta*. New York: United Nations.

UNDP. (2007). Human Development Index Report. http://hdrstats.undp.org/countries/country_fact_sheets/cty_fs_MMR.html. Accessed 5 Dec 2008.

UNHCR (United Nations High Commissioner for Refugees). (2001). *Statistical Yearbook 2001*. Geneva: UNHCR.

UNHCR. (2002). *Guidelines on international protection: Gender-related persecution within the context of Article 1A(2) of the 1951 convention and/or its 1967 protocol relating to the status of refugees*. Geneva: UNHCR.

UNHCR. (2005). *UNHCR deplores excessive force at peaceful demonstration, welcomes prompt government enquiry*. Geneva: UNHCR.

UNHCR. (2007a). *The detention of refugees and asylum-seekers by reason of their unauthorised entry or presence*. Rome: UNHCR.

UNHCR. (2007b). *Statistical Yearbook*. Geneva: UNHCR.

UNHCR. (2008). *Global trends*. Geneva: UNHCR.

UNHCR. (2010). 2010 regional operations profile: Northern, western and southern Europe. http://www.unhcr.org/pages/49e48eba6.html. Accessed 18 Jan 2010.

UNICEF. (2010). Statistics on Myanmar. (Updated March 2, 2010). http://www.unicef.org/infoby-country/myanmar_statistics.html#58.

UNODC (United Nations Office on Drugs & Crime). (2004). Protocol to Prevent, Suppress and Punish Trafficking in Persons, Especially Women and Children, supplementing the United Nations Convention against Transnational Organized Crime Status Report. http://www.unodc.org/unodc/en/crime_cicp_signatures.html.

UNODC. (2010a). United Nations Convention against Transnational Organized Crime and its Protocols. http://www.unodc.org/unodc/en/treaties/CTOC/index.html.

UNODC. (2010b). Report on Myanmar. http://www.unodc.org/eastasiaandpacific/en/topics/illicit-trafficking/index.html.

UNSD. (2008). Millennium Development Goals Indicators: The official United Nations site for the MDG Indicators. Millennium Development Goals Indicators. http://mdgs.un.org/unsd/mdg/data.aspx. Accessed 24 Sept 2009.

US Committee for Refugees and Immigrants (USCRI). (2009). 2009 Report. http://www.refugees.org.

USDOS. (2002). Trafficking in Persons Report. http://www.state.gov/g/tip/rls/tiprpt/2002/

USDOS. (2004). Trafficking in Persons Report. http://www.state.gov/g/tip/rls/tiprpt/2004/index.htm.

USDOS. (2005). Trafficking in Persons Report. http://www.state.gov/g/tip/rls/tiprpt/2005/index.htm.

USDOS. (2006). Trafficking in Persons Report. http://www.state.gov/g/tip/rls/tiprpt/2006/index.htm.

USDOS. (2007). Trafficking in Persons Report. http://www.state.gov/g/tip/rls/tiprpt/2007/index.htm.

USDOS. (2008). Trafficking in Persons Report. http://www.state.gov/g/tip/rls/tiprpt/2009/index.htm.

USDOS. (2009). Trafficking in Persons Report. http://www.state.gov/g/tip/rls/tiprpt/2009/index.htm.

USDOS. (2010). Trafficking in Persons Report. http://www.state.gov/g/tip/rls/tiprpt/2010/index.htm.

Weber, C. (1995). *Simulating sovereignty*. Cambridge: Cambridge University Press.

Weber, L. (2006). The shifting frontiers of migration control. In S. Pickering & L. Weber (Eds.), *Borders, mobility and technologies of control* (pp. 21–44). New York: Springer.

Weber, L., & Gelsthorpe, L. (2000). *Deciding to detain: How decisions to detain asylum seekers are made at ports of entry*. Cambridge: Institute of Criminology, University of Cambridge.

Weber, L., & Bowling, B. (2004). Policing migration: An international framework for investigating the regulation of global mobility, *Policing and Society, 14*(3), 195–212.

Williams, K. (2003, March 13). How a girl's dream of freedom died. *The Daily Telegraph*, p. 2.

Wonders, N. (2006). Global flows, semi-permeable borders and new channels of inequality. In S. Pickering & L. Weber (Eds.), *Borders, mobility and technologies of control* (pp. 63–86). New York: Springer.

Wynhausen, E. (2003a, March 13). Sick and alone…tragic end for a sex slave. *The Australian*, p. 3.

Wynhausen, E. (2003b, 7 June). Parents deny selling daughter. *The Weekend Australian*, p. 9.

Young, J. (2007). *The vertigo of late modernity*. London: Sage.

Index